WAY OF THE VIOLENT

Printed in the United States of America

First Printing, 2021

ISBN 978-0-578-76513-6

Salt Churches

WAY OF THE VIOLENT
WAY OF THE VIOLENT

By Parker R. Green

ENDORSEMENTS

I've had the joy of getting to know Parker and Jessi Green, not simply from a distance or watching them through media, but actually sitting with the Greens for meals and fellowship, praying with them, and seeing their passion for Jesus in demonstration (on the beaches in Southern CA). Parker carries a fire that reminds me of Tozer or Ravenhill, two pioneers who would never have called themselves prophets, but they were perhaps more prophetic than many of the self-proclaimed "prophets" today. Why? They burned with a message of the restoration of true, Biblical Christianity. May this book ignite your heart with that same consuming fire for Jesus—not some "god" we have fashioned in our own image, but rather, a vision of the true God from Scripture, a vision that undoes you, a vision that motivates you, and a vision that calls you into your assignment to represent Heaven on Earth.

Larry Sparks
Publisher Destiny Image

The first book in a long time that whenever I put it down, I wanted to pick it back up. It is confronting and challenging but also inspiring and empowering. One of my prayers for this generation is that the church would never be so safe that no one gets set free. This book is like fuel on the coals of that prayer. It's time for the people of God to make a stand, and this book just might be the whip to get us moving.

Joel Ramsey
Pastor Citipointe Church, Nashville,
Founder: Gospel Goodness

The Way of the Violent will challenge you on your personal view of Jesus and help you to live out your faith in ways that are practical and powerful in your everyday life. Parker is courageous in the way he lives and shares his faith and this is reflected in his bold approach to reshaping how churches are done. Parker is forging out a new way for the church to grow and be discipled through SALT churches, breaking away from norms and looking to expand the church through leaving the mega model and focusing on the micro. This new medium allows for others to experience a deeper sense of community and connection. It takes a bold person to lead in a way that demands sacrifice and calls for change but it is only from this place one can cultivate something new.

Scott Bakken
Creative Director @scottbakken

Dedicated to my wife.

Whose violence of heart plunders the enemy of our souls;
and has inspired so many to do the same.

CONTENTS

ACKNOWLEDGEMENTS

To my wife, who I dedicated this book to. For never letting me become a domesticated house husband. For dealing with the late nights of writing this book over the last few years, and believing that men should be men.

I would like to thank my parents. For raising me right and for staying together despite a literal walk through hell.

Paul Andrew, who saw ministry on my life when I was an arrogant and obnoxious, but somewhat likeable, 14 year old.

Clint Bokelman, who challenged me to step into the fire of discipleship from the perspective of a missionary and a prophet.

And my boys, David and Ethan, I hope this book helps shape a better world for you to grow up in.

To Dallas Willard, whom I never knew and who is with the Lord now, for opening my eyes to the reality that I could really live like Jesus, and could really see the Kingdom of the Heavens today. Your book, "The Divine Conspiracy" forever altered the course of my life.

To Joe and David, two of the men I disciple and who disciple others. They are walking this out as well and I know they will have stories of their own to share with the world soon.

I'd like to thank Caleb Alba who generously and zealously offered to design this book. Without his help I do not know what

I would have done. And to Edie, my editor, you were paid far too little to help with this book and your suggestions shaped the message to a great degree.

And so many who have been kind to me when I haven't deserved it, loved me when I needed it desperately, and cut me with words so brutal and healing at the same time. Thank you.

FOREWORD

"To make a fighter you gotta strip them down to bare wood: you can't just tell 'em to forget everything you know if you gotta make 'em forget even their bones... make 'em so tired they only listen to you, only hear your voice, only do what you say and nothing else... show 'em how to keep their balance and take it away from the other guy... how to generate momentum off their right toe and how to flex your knees when you fire a jab... how to fight backin' up so that the other guy doesn't want to come after you. Then you gotta show 'em all over again. Over and over and over... till they think they're born that way." —Eddie Scrap-Iron Dupris, trainer

In the movie, *Million Dollar Baby*, Eddie Scrap describes the making of a fighter by stripping them down to *"bare wood."* This is an incredible illustration of why the Church has lost so many good men. We have forgotten the art of discipleship- the art of stripping men and women down, only to build them back up in Christ. Unfortunately, we have stepped away from the Matthew 28 mandate to make disciples that Jesus gave us over 2,000 years ago.

In his book, *Way of the Violent*, Parker tackles the harsh reality of an emasculated Church in America, one whom has walked away from intimacy with Jesus and abandoning her once held *"storm the gates of hell"* conviction.

He strips the reader down to *"bare wood."* He teaches men how to take the kingdom of God by force and how to pursue Godly passion. And like fighters who learns to *"keep their balance and take it away from the other guy,"* Parker deconstructs the enemy's plan to take you out.

He reasons through why we need more lions in the Church. The Church was never meant to be a safe haven for men. The lion engages culture, is in the fight, and will fight to the death. Parker reveals what it is to be men who walk in the ways of Jesus through an intimate relationship with the Creator of heaven and earth, and to fight as the roaring lion.

"If you say what Jesus said and do what Jesus did, you will get what Jesus got." —Troy Johnson

Parker tells the hard of what Jesus said, the strength of what He did, and prepares men for the same treatment we are sure to get. Carefully outlined within these pages, is the Gospel, the Good News of Christ's death, burial, and resurrection. The simplicity of the Gospel is the power of the Gospel. This is the real Jesus to whom real men respond. Not the portrait of a less-than-masculine Jesus holding the lamb on His shoulders, you know the one- but a true picture of the Man whose life was marked by this perfect dance between love and power, kindness and authority, mercy and grit.

Parker vividly expresses the visceral response in which God has created all men to walk- one that can taste the blood of a beaten Jesus tethered to man's rejection, which fuels *"full-tilt rebellion against the ways of the world and all the cheap imitations of the world."*

Prior to pastoring for the last 24 years, I played professional ice hockey for ten. The greatest misconception of being a Christian hockey player is that you're soft—that this loving Jesus you serve would never approve of this violent game. And don't even get me started with fighting in hockey, Jesus would never allow that! I would regularly play to prove that wasn't true by being the hardest worker every time I stepped on the ice, or starting a fight when I needed another player to understand I wasn't going to put up with his crap!

You see, the Jesus I was introduced to at an early age was the one whom Parker gives sight to throughout this book. He introduces you to *"Meek Jesus,"* the Jesus many men have never met. The world has hijacked the word meek and made it mean only *"weak."* A weak man is perhaps one with hunched shoulders who won't look you in the eye, who lacks confidence and allows others to walk all over him, but that's not Jesus. The truth is the word meek means *"strength under control."*

Strength under control—the secret sauce to every great athlete. Micheal Jordan, Tom Brady, Wayne Gretzky—all had an incredible strength they used at exactly the perfect moments, and those moments produced championships.

The championship that Parker is calling us to has less to do with titles and rings and more to do with being the husband, father and friend God has called us to be. It's about men who are willing to engage in the fight... fights for purity and honesty and truth. It's a life which chooses to violently say *"No"* to the world and all that it has to offer, dying to the flesh every single day, and allowing Jesus to direct every step.

William Wallace, in one of the most formidable moments prior to battle, against the more powerful, more knowledgeable, and the greatest fighting force in the world at that time, challenges his men with these words...

"Aye, fight and you may die. Run, and you'll live... at least a while. And dying in your beds, many years from now, would you be willin' to trade ALL the days, from this day to that, for one chance, just one chance, to come back here and tell our enemies that they may take our lives, but they'll never take... OUR FREEDOM!"

What a great illustration for the fight every man is called to in this life. It is in the middle of the fight that you feel alive! It's in the battle that you discover who God has created you to be. God has placed in every man a heart to defend and come to the aid of; however we are constantly choosing the wrong skirmishes. Parker takes us on a journey that shows us the real & right fights worth engaging daily. He calls men to walk in the fullness of who God has called them to be without compromising their manhood. Jesus was a man's man, and He has called you and I to be men of God, as well.

Before you start to read this book, take some time to pray and ask God to prepare your heart. Ask the Holy Spirit to reveal to you where you have abdicated your role as a man—where you have stepped aside and allowed others to lead where God has called you to lead.

Come with an expectant heart, watch what He might do, and go conquer the mountain!

John Blue
Former NHL goalie turned Church planter
Pacific Point Church, Costa Mesa, CA

INTRODUCTION

The Heart of the Matter

rev·o·lu·tion revəˈloॖoSH(ə)n/ noun

a forcible overthrow of a government or social order in
favor of a new system.

How did Jesus start a revolution—or should I say—*the* revolution?

How did a band of about 120 disciples of Jesus go from hiding in a room with the doors locked to turning the world upside down?

So often, I've been obsessed with *what* the men and women did in the book of Acts while skipping over *why* they did what they did. I've been reading the book by Simon Sinek, *Start With Why.*[1] Let's just say it has been challenging. I'm looking at the apostles, and myself, in a whole new light.

What was the apostles' *why?* Why did the world get turned upside down? Why did people walk into repentance and get baptized at alarming rates?

We get stoked on a 10 percent rate of increase in church attendance while on the very first day of the church, by the power of the Holy Spirit, the number of believers went from 120 to about 5,120. That's like a 4,000 percent increase!

Some people, namely the original 120, *really, genuinely believed.* That belief was heard and acted upon to the point where the people in the crowd at Pentecost said, *"What must we do?!"*

And the response was mass baptism and repentance.

Why, then, did these 120 believe so deeply?

Because *a dead man became a living man.* That same power of the living Man was poured out onto and into these 120 followers of Jesus at Pentecost. Literally, the same life flowed through their bodies that flowed through Christ.

I want that! *People will believe that.* I want that *why.* I want a living Jesus, not one I must manipulate people to meet or convince them of His reality.

The thing with living people is they tend to turn up or show up and, most definitely, *act out.*

So, how do you start a revolution?

You overthrow the system of death and replace it with a system of life. You come back from the dead and then share the same power that accomplished the defeat of death with your followers.

Why follow Jesus?

He's alive.

Why read my Bible?

He's alive.

Why become a part of a group of believers?

He's alive.

Why does the Sermon on the Mount matter?

He's alive.

Why repent?

He's alive.

Why be baptized?

He's alive.

Why share the gospel with everyone you possibly can?

He's alive.

Why be filled with the Holy Spirit?

He's alive

dis·ci·ple dəˈsīpəl/ noun

a personal follower of Jesus during his life, especially one of the twelve Apostles.

Why make disciples?

He's alive.

You'll notice above that the Webster's definition of disciple states, *"during his life."* Well, I see what you tried to do there, Webster, but He's alive!

A living Jesus is our reason. In order to perpetuate this revolution, we must carry that same life in us--the life of the Spirit of Christ or the Holy Spirit. Ask God to baptize you with the Holy Spirit consistently for a week and see what happens.

Now, how do you start a religion?

You lose your living Savior. His life becomes an idea just short of your reality. Then you start to manipulate into programs, routines, ritual, and argument because, when the why is gone, there is only manipulation left.

Here are some blaring examples of manipulation when the why goes out the window. You'll notice that businesses use the same names of the types stolen from Simon Sinek:[2]

"All you have to do is say a prayer"—Cost reduction

"Pray this prayer and you'll be rich"—Aspiration

"Read your Bible and you'll be a better person"—Aspiration

"If you don't come to this, you'll get a phone call or a text"—Fear

"Listen to this new song/podcast"—Novelty

"Guest speaker today!"—Promotion

These things aren't inherently wrong, except for a couple of them. I'll let you and the Almighty decide which ones those are. But if you use this as your approach to discipleship, you are on a hamster wheel of disappointment—almost guaranteed.

When the why is genuine, the outcome will be genuine action.

People respond to that.

They'll wait in line for that.

They'll fill a house to the point where there is no room for that. Note the ministry of Jesus. Just look at the result of Jesus' work in Mark 1:29–34:

> *As soon as they left the synagogue, they went with James and John to the home of Simon and Andrew. Simon's moth-er-in-law was in bed with a fever, and they immediately told Jesus about her. So he went to her, took her hand and helped her up. The fever left her and she began to wait on them. That evening after sunset the people brought to Jesus all the sick and demon-possessed. The whole town gathered at the door, and Jesus healed many who had various diseases. He also drove out many demons, but he would not let the demons speak because they knew who he was.*

Ask yourself this question: *Why am I doing this Christianity thing?* Let the Holy Spirit and the Word lead you. It might change everything. It just might provoke you to something radical that results in violent action—violence that takes the Kingdom by force—and that, in turn, will bring revolution.

THE SANITIZATION OF A SAVIOR

"From the days of John the Baptist until now the kingdom of heaven suffers violence, and violent men take it by force."

—Jesus of Nazareth

The Bible is violent. It likely doesn't help that so much of the stories told took place during the Bronze Age, when life was far more brutal and cruel, at least it's judged so to the modern, Westerner.

As you can imagine, before I really started reading the Bible for myself, as a young boy, I was far more interested in the stories where people killed each other. David, oh man, he was the guy who killed the giant with a sling! I didn't find out until later, though, that he also cut off the giant's head with the giant's own sword, killed Philistines all day that day, soaked in their blood, and then he took the head back to the king and got tax exemption for himself and his family for life! Wow!

The other night, I was reading a bedtime story to my son. He's a year old. His name? David, of course. The story I was reading to David was about a father taking his son to the top of a mountain to sacrifice him to God. The story is the story of Abraham. He was commanded by God to take his only son whom he loved to the top of a mountain to sacrifice him. Luckily, God jumped in at the last moment and said, *"Don't worry about it. I know you love Me now. Behold, a ram in a thicket for you to sacrifice."* We then narrowly avoid human sacrifice committed by the great fore-father of our faith. *"Whew, that was close, God. You were almost crazy."* But wait, there's more in the Bible that we teach our kids!

Let's not forget our favorite childhood story, the flood, or more affectionately known as *"Noah's Ark."* Just a few thousand ani-mals and a family escaped death when God flooded the earth and destroyed all of its inhabitants. But we neglect to think about all the other animals. What did they do? What happened to them? Or what about the other people who didn't get to go on the ark?

Think of the terror of families drowning, of people having no dry land to put their feet on no matter where they swam or floundered. Yet, we decorate our nurseries with this traumatic illustration, making it look as if it's one happy time on a floating zoo headed for a beautiful rainbow. We fail to recognize the *re-ality* of the Bible. Yes, the narrative and metaphor are absolutely crucial, but we believe these things really happened.

Thankfully, these stories are not what the entirety of the Bible is about, but I bring them up to make a point. As a society, we have whitewashed the Bible completely clean of its humanity to make ourselves comfortable with the utter violence, grittiness, and sin *(gasp)* that overflow from its pages. In fact, we have even whitewashed all the Arabs, Persians, and Jews—the people who were farming and empire building before the Europeans had started leaving their caves.

The Bible is an intensely human book and also a divine book. It's a hard balance to maintain in your head because it's actually not a balance at all. *It is completely both human and divine.* After all, the Word of God has to be. It has to be a story we can connect to, and it has to be holy, or there is no place for us to go or run to. In fact, the Bible, in all the craziness and absolute miracles that allowed us to hold it in our hands, is a perfect guide to a person, to the Person.

The entire narrative of Scripture, the whole story, points toward Christ—completely divine, completely human. I think it's important to remember that we shouldn't measure which He had more of, like a 50/50 split down the middle of humanity and divinity—half God, half man. He's not some Hercules from Greco-Roman mythology. He is God made flesh, not a demigod here to help you out a little bit.

100 percent and 100 percent is the best way to look at it that I can think of. Jesus lived on the earth, He peed, He pooped, He sweated, He slept, He got hungry, and He got tired. He also opened blind eyes, healed the sick, raised the dead, forgave sins, cast out demons, and calmed storms. But that's not how He's always presented.

I remember sitting in kids' ministry as a five- or six-year-old. We were in a small church, or maybe a cult—maybe a church and a cult, not so sure what to call it—and the adults would come downstairs on rotation to help out. We would all gather around a little felt board, and characters from the Bible would be placed on it as a story was told. I remember specifically what Jesus looked like—long flowing brown hair, blue eyes, and a perfect blue sash to match. It was like Jesus was the winner of a Messiah of the Universe beauty pageant. The guy was clean, always acted nicely (even when casting out demons), and was so soft, literally and figuratively.

I Need the Real Jesus

When I first got married, my wife planned a camping trip for me on the Fourth of July right after my birthday. If you know my wife, you know she does not camp and had not camped up to that point. Planning this all out and finding the spot was a huge deal for her and a great loving gesture, I might add. Guess what, though?

I was a total jerk! All the logistics of actually carrying all the stuff around (we lived in New York City at the time) and getting to the camping stuff no longer felt like a gift. It felt like a burden. So, I fumed in our tiny little apartment, said some wildly angry things, then kicked a hole through one of our cabinets. I realized at that moment that something wasn't working. I had a made-up Jesus in my head who seemed to never disagree with me and was failing me all the time. Then I realized, *Wait a second, my god is me!* That's why he's such a terrible God! I had made Jesus me and me Jesus, and so what I supposed was me being a good follower of Jesus really was just the religion of me; and it failed me at every turn.

I needed Jesus. The real one. The flesh-and-blood one, but also the God Jesus. How could I possibly trust a pale-faced, soft-handed, flimsy, nice guy who had been so often presented to me in a more *"approachable"* way?

I felt I needed to make Jesus up in my own head in order to follow Him. This was the point at which the gospel of Jesus got one more shot with me.

I opened up Matthew and decided I would only read Matthew, Mark, Luke, and John for the next three months. What I found was a Jesus whom I had never really experienced before. I'm not exactly sure what it was that opened my eyes or why it was so radically different this time. Maybe, this time, there were no assumptions that I already knew who He was. There was a searching in my heart that I just had not felt in years—an open world and the impetuous curiosity of a child. I did my level best to read the stories of the Gospels like I'd never laid eyes on them before, like they were intended initially—stories of the Man who claimed to be the Messiah, the Savior of the world, who died, then came back from the dead. It was the story of a brand new Kingdom, or perhaps one I had never heard of before, with a man at the helm whom I could trust and respect, even deeply love.

There was so much more than the caricature that religion had sanitized for my comfort and yours—than what I call the *consumer Christianity*. I read that, yes, Jesus does love me, even to death, but I also read that He is alive and well and truly in charge. He's the Boss with no rivals whatsoever. I read about a Jesus who used His strength to lift up the severely broken and then turned and tore into the religious elite, in public and on purpose. This Jesus was picking fights. I read about a Jesus who invested heavily into a few men, loved them, rebuked them brutally, and made open displays of awesome power for them to see.

This was a man I could follow. He was a why I could embrace. What an incredible world I would soon discover.

A VIOLENT PASSION

"Oh! precious is the flow / That makes me white as snow; / No other fount I know, / Nothing but the blood of Jesus."

—*Robert Lowry, "Nothing But the Blood of Jesus"*

There are few things that bring me to tears, not because I am unemotional or don't feel deep sadness, but because I just am not a big crier. Perhaps I would be better off if I did have a good cry now and again, but that is beside my point for now.

Whenever I sing the song, *"Nothing but the Blood,"* I can't help but begin to cry when I see Jesus in my mind's eye choose to bleed and die for me while I still was against Him with every fiber of my being. When I was rebelling against Him and knew better, when my sorrow overwhelmed me from my own foolish sin and poor decision making, there it was—His blood poured out for me. It was enough to wash me of every single thing I had done wrong and every wrong I was going to do. This kind of love was so unfamiliar to me, I simply could not wrap my head around it. So, I allowed my heart to surrender to it.

The first time I got truly saved, when my life turned around, I was a weeping young man in the shower who had a badly broken heart. I knew *of* Christ, I had heard of His power to save, but I had never actually felt the presence of God surround me or the tangible realization that His blood was enough for whatever ailed me.

I remember some vague words I cried out to Him while on my knees, with the false anonymity of the shower and its soothing heat running over my head. I was begging God, pleading with Jesus, to take away my pain, to be my Lord. I had realized my way was not the Way. In that moment, I felt a stillness I can't even explain to this day. Even my own internal voice was silenced by the authority that had suddenly entered the room. I knew that Jesus was there. His presence was nearer than the words I had just spoken, and I could literally feel Him washing the refuse off me. The God of heaven and the earth had found His wandering son, wallowing in his own filth and starving to death, and He took pity. Thank you, Jesus. Jesus took pity on me. It was in that moment when I really knew what the passion of the Christ really was.

It was not just an act of the Son of God in history, but it had been acted upon me in that moment. The blood and the cross and the resurrection all converged on a teenager in a shower, crying out to Jesus. The kind of love that I was looking for had found me, and it did not shift its gaze. Uncomfortable as that may seem, I was seen for who I really was, naked in a couple of ways, and completely loved, accepted, and without defense. This is what gave me the ability to repent and turn toward Jesus. I required change. I could see the contrast so clearly between my sin and His goodness that all I could do was say, *"You're in charge now, and I trust You."*

This is when I got saved. This is when I felt what Jesus had done for me in that present moment.

You see, many people understand the historical relevance of the cross of Jesus. They understand that a man died and that He rose again. Many of these people would even call themselves Christians. To experience the blood of Jesus' with its transformative power, though, is a universe away from having a vague idea about a man who died for you and lives to reign over all the affairs of heaven and Earth, which includes your individual life as well. Yes, Jesus is Lord of your life—in charge, as it were. Jesus can only be your friend as much as He is your Lord *first.*

Think of it like this. When you walk into a grocery store and buy a ribeye, you probably aren't thinking about the process that got it into your cart and on to your table. You likely don't think, *I wonder what this cow's name was, probably Moomoo, or Steely, or something. Thank you for your sacrifice, cow.* My guess is that most meat that you buy just goes down your little gullet without a care in the world as to how it got there. You know what, that's fine, kind of. The issue starts when this kind of "well it's on my plate now so who cares" attitude relates to other things in your life. Anyone can recite a prayer, acknowledging that Jesus died for their sins, anyone. Even the demons of hell and the devil himself know that this is factually true, although, unfortunately, they aren't off the hook.

The difference between knowing that Jesus died for you and

experiencing the reality of His blood and resurrection to change your life is like the difference between buying a steak all neat and wrapped at a grocery store and a family farmer cutting open a cow on a Friday afternoon for dinner that weekend.

The death of Jesus has been so sanitized that we end up with this feeling of, *Did He really mean it? Was it really that hard? Does it matter for me today?*

It becomes extraordinarily difficult to experience the love of Jesus when we don't realize what He has really done for us—what the passion of the Christ really means in our everyday lives. Chances are, tomorrow you will not see a crucifixion. Likely, you will never see one except for in a movie. Then, sometimes, something even worse can happen. What we see on the screen can get grouped in with every other mythical tale that we take in on the big screen. *"Wow, that movie made me cry." "I got so emotional." "I got so convicted."* The message of Jesus' crucifixion can become like another Sunday message that you listen to and do nothing about. So, what has to change for us to experience the violent love of Jesus?

It has to become personal. As C. S. Lewis said, *"He died not for men, but for each man. If each man had been the only man made, He would have done no less."*[1]

Yes, Jesus did die for the restoration of humankind. Yet, He also died for *you.*

The only way to transform us all was to transform us one at a time. This is unbearably uncomfortable to dwell upon for very

long, especially if for a second you thought you had this all fig-
ured out and especially if you knew that Jesus loved you and all
that. But if He were looking right at you and telling you, *"I died
for you. My eternal blood, poured out in Judea two thousand or so
years ago, that was for you and you alone in a completely unique
way."* Now, you would be transformed by that.

That's the real problem we face. When we experience this love,
this absolutely violent and literally blood-soaked love, *we have to
change.* But not because we *"have to"* in all its irony, but because
we will be overwhelmed with the desire to be transformed by
this Man who died for us, who died brutally, alone. He was the
Man who died for you and me as individuals, so you and I as
individuals can be changed. And, therefore, the world can be
changed.

Jesus died for—wait for it—*you!* And you don't want simply to
shrug it off as something somebody puts up on a church building or on a T-shirt. But just think about the madness of this
for one second. No, meditate on this. In fact, take five minutes
right now and think about the fact that someone is willing to
die for you. That this someone is also a king. That this someone
is the King of kings and is enthroned in heaven and *physically
worshipped.* I am talking about someone who lovingly and com-
petently manages the affairs of the universe. *This Person,* He is
the one who made the choice to die for you so that you could be
restored to right relationship with Him and to those around you.

The difference between the sacrifice of Jesus and every other
sacrifice in all of time is that He was the only option available to

actually remove you from your sin, that He willingly and lovingly took pity on you and decided to die for you. He died for you while you hated Him; perhaps not always with your words, but with your actions, you ignored God, and while you did so, He sacrificed for you.

Just knowing that this act of love was done on your behalf is transformative enough if you really truly and deeply believe it. We must take it a step further, however, because Jesus does not love us in a *"just enough"* kind of way. The blood that He shed makes it possible for us to be restored in relationship with Him. Now you may have heard this preached from a thousand pulpits before, but it only has so little effect because you don't believe Jesus is who He says He is.

This relationship, with Jesus as our Lord, changes all the possibilities in our lives. We are no longer destined to defeat, despair, depression, brokenness, bitterness, resentment, addiction, or anything like these things. We are now in the family of the King. He doesn't die so we can have a nice place to sleep in the yard just outside the palace. *"Well, dude, I saved you, and that should be good enough."* Indeed, it would be, but that is not how Jesus loves us at all.

The passion of Jesus Christ, His physically dying for you on a cross and then coming back to life is the single most brazen act of overwhelming love in the history of the world. Not one religion, sacrifice, or philosophy can come close to this, or even close to explaining it away.

It must be described as violent. It must be described as relentless.

It must be described as overwhelming.

Violent, relentless, overwhelming *love*—this is not squishy, rom-com, love for the day, hook up for the night, let's live together to *"try it out"* kind of love. This is the kind of love that echoes like unceasing cannon fire through the annals of history and yet has a perfect tune and harmony for every individual who would answer its call.

We cannot help but be changed by this. Our change will be evident and will change others.

> *When you were dead in your sins and in the uncircumcision of your flesh, God made you alive with Christ. He forgave us all our sins, having canceled the charge of our legal indebtedness, which stood against us and condemned us; he has taken it away, nailing it to the cross. And having disarmed the powers and authorities, he made a public spectacle of them, triumphing over them by the cross.* (Colossians 2:13–15)

Jesus makes a public spectacle of your enemies—depression, loneliness, addiction, lust, anger, and sin of every kind!

Jesus made a public display on the cross. Your enemies are defeated.

The question remains: Will you be able to accept the kind of love that He offers? When you do, it will change you, and you will likely lose control of your own life. Is that what you are prepared to do? To receive the kind of love, in the end, that will kill the parts of you that were dead anyway?

We talk a lot about being born again, but if you have experienced the birth of a child, labor isn't some sterile pretty process. Bringing life into this world literally requires love that's prepared to pay any price. If you want to be born again by the Spirit, the violent love of Jesus will kill the things that imprison you. Let me tell you a secret, though. You will discover that the things you give up—the things that die, even the parts of your identity that pass through the fire and the blood—weren't worth half a penny buried at the bottom of a septic tank compared to the resurrection life you receive.

To receive Jesus, we must receive all of Him. There is no part of Jesus we can nestle into a neat little corner of our lives, no Jesus jacket we can take on and off in different crowds and Jesus is my pal and sometimes He comes. You take all, or you take none.

This isn't because Jesus is unfair or unjust. It's simply the fact that He is a person who died for you. What kind of lunatic would accept only part of what someone said that died and then rose again so that *you could have life?*

Love like that is beyond compelling. It's revolutionary, and I am of the opinion that it should start one both in you and the world around you.

Jesus does call us to follow Him in this way—to die so that we can live. But only because He loves us so much that He did it first. There is nothing that Jesus commands that He hasn't done Himself. If anything at all is refreshing, I hope that this fact is. Sure, He asks us to die daily and carry a cross, but He did those things first, and He showed us clearly that resurrection power is on the other end.

If you haven't already, will you receive Jesus in the way that He presents Himself? Not just as an historical character, but as a present reality in your life? As the King who died for you and beckons you to follow, to die, and to be reborn in Him?

It's not easy to receive this kind of love, but I promise it's what you've been looking for: *"For whoever wants to save their life will lose it, but whoever loses their life for me will find it'"* (Matthew 16:25).

YOU DON'T GET CRUCIFIED FOR BEING "NICE"

"The Gospel is like a caged lion. It does not need to be defended, it simply needs to be let out of its cage"

—*Charles Spurgeon*

Idolatry is a funny thing. No, really, it is if you think about it. We all have idols, and they are all stupid and fail us. But let me say it again in case you were shocked by my using the word stupid: We all have had or do have idols. Plain and simple.

Here is a fun example of an idol in my life.

I am a pretty physically strong person. I like picking up heavy things and putting them down, many times, repeatedly until I feel sick. One day, when I pulled a deadlift bar (physically picking a bar up and putting it down) from the ground, my back said, *"Hey! I've been here all this time, and you never call anymore,"* and I couldn't breathe from the excruciating pain shooting up and down my back. My idol of personal physical strength took quite the tumble that day.

Seven to eight years prior, I had broken or cracked a couple ver-
tebra. I had rebuilt my strength and could perform many exer-
cises I wasn't supposed to be able to. I basically thought I was
better than folks who didn't share my false dreams of purely
physical masculinity. That being said, the deadlift incident severely hampered my ability to go to the level I desired to in my
training. I even experienced some fun tingling in my left leg on
occasion. What I realized after this experience was my idol was
me. I know that sounds funny, but check yourself out. You just
may be your own idol. And if so, this is why our god fails us
so much—it fails because our idol is us! We make ourselves into
little gods and call that god over there, Jesus, or Christianity,
or whatever. When we pray, we pray to a made-up Jesus in our
heads that's a lot like us.

Now, God is extremely patient with us, considering how unbelievably powerful He is. This is why I think that the *"me god"*
failing to come through for you in life is one of the best possible
things that could happen to you. It was for me anyway.

I was in extraordinary amounts of pain at times with my injury.
I am not saying God made this happen, but I feel like He might
have giggled a little when I began realizing how finite my ability was to control and change the world around me, let alone
change my own body. You know, the whole *"you can't even make
one hair on your head white or black"* kind of thing. I'm embar-
rassed to admit, let alone write, how much the deadlift injury
worked me over at a deeply emotional level.

Jesus, or some random version of who Jesus was supposed to be, was my idol. I took a long hard look at my life in reverse, and I had a funny thought. It reminded me of that poster that is always up over grandma's toilet. It's called *"Footprints."* The poem on the poster basically says, when the person in the poem gets to heaven and looks back on his life, he asks God why he sees only one set of footprints, and the Lord responds, *"That is when I carried you."* How nice. The man, now in heaven, was never alone on the earth. In a sense, this is very true.

Now, when I think of this poem, I know it is absolutely correct in one sense. Jesus is absolutely with us and loves us unconditionally. Many times, though, He will let us crawl to discover our false god is not Him at all so that we cry out to Him. This is when *He carries us and heals us to walk in power.* But that healing comes to us in ways that may be surprising to us. For that matter, how Jesus heals us, whom He uses, and what He may tell us to do may shock us. We have to remember how unbelievably offensive Jesus was, especially to those who thought of themselves as morally superior. The weight of pride that we sometimes carry is the very weight Jesus will use to break us so that He can actually use us.

"Get Up!"

Take the man at the pool of Bethesda, for example. *"When Jesus saw him lying there and learned that he had been in this condition for a long time, he asked him, 'Do you want to get well?'"* (John 5:6 NKJV). This guy had been sitting next to a magic pool and had tried to crawl in it and get healed for years! Then Jesus strolled up and had the nerve to ask this man, *"Do you want to get healed?"*

"Really, Jesus? What do You think?"

The man's response is funny considering who he was talking to. *"'Sir,' the invalid replied, 'I have no one to help me into the pool when the water is stirred. While I am trying to get in, someone else goes down ahead of me'"* (John 5:7 NKJV). The guy threw up an excuse. *"I can't move, obviously, so the guy who has some other disease that allows him to walk gets in before me."*

Now, Jesus' response changed everything, and I think we take this for granted. "Jesus said to him, 'Get up! Pick up your mat and walk.' At once the man was cured; he picked up his mat and walked" (John 5:8–9).

The man was healed!

"All right! Good job, Jesus."

But look at how Jesus talked to the man. He shouted at him, *"Get up! Pick up your mat and walk."* We have to realize that this radically changed the life of the man. No more begging, no more *"woe is me,"* nor more victimhood. He would have to get a job to replace his lost income that he used to receive from begging.

This man was relying on his own strength to get to God when God showed up in the flesh, and kind of, well, healed him whether he liked it or not. You don't hear any confession of faith or any real faith at all from the man, only complaints and concerns. Jesus took pity on the man and his condition and healed him anyway.

Isn't it funny how much Jesus is obsessed with us while we lay next to a pool of religion, hoping it will heal us? All the while, our crippled religion won't get us there. Jesus comes to us and asks us the real question, *"Do you want to be healed?"*

Is it depression? Anxiety? Addiction? Grief? Confusion? Cancer? There are things men and the systems of men, religious and otherwise, simply cannot do. Only a real Jesus can. All we have to do is accept that fact, His pity, and His grace for our situation.

I think I know what my little beach walk in the sand looked like. The poem is not quite so pretty, yet it could be seen as poetic in its eventual outcome. *"See that, Parker, where the footprints sprinted into the ocean? That was when you were a teenager. That was stupid. You almost drowned. See that over there? That's your mid-twenties. They're just some heel marks from where you were getting dragged because you drank more booze than was preferable for a professed follower of Jesus."*

"But, Lord, You carried me!

"No that wasn't Me. You weren't following Me. It was someone to whom you had ascribed My name, so he was kind of like an imaginary friend."

"Wait. What, Jesus?"

"Yes, most of the marks on the sand are when you were flailing around trying to make sense of everything. I was there, though, and

funny thing is you knew in your heart I was there all along. The way you grew up, the access you had to who I am was really unparalleled in history. The problem was I wouldn't let your imaginary friend live, and you had to be transformed. Of course, all by My grace, but you had to change, nonetheless. You had to die, and then I'd bring you back to life, only different."

The real Jesus saved me after all! After all my flailing after other gods and trying to *"do my thing,"* He was the one who asked me, *"Do you want to be healed?"*

My answer was an emphatic, *"What exactly do You mean?"*

By His grace, He's healed me anyway. Jesus literally saved me from myself. I was the god of my own life, and He crushed that god to dust yet with compassion. It was His compassion and love toward me that made me fear His power. Who in their right mind would have all the power of the universe and take pity on someone so rebellious toward him? There is no one, no one, in heaven or on the earth like Jesus.

This little version of *Pilgrim's Progress* that played in my head showed me one thing. I had made Jesus *"mine,"* as in I had made Him another one of my possessions in my self-absorbed consumerism. Obviously, it had miserably failed me. Jesus could never belong to me in this sense because He is God, Lord, Leader, Redeemer, Teacher, Alpha, Omega, the Guy who runs the universe and spoke it into being. This Jesus—the real one, the one who could change me—could not be contained in my religiosity, in my church, or even in my perception of reality.

I had taken some hodge-podge portions of Jesus that assimilated well with my personality so that I never really had to do what He asked in the Gospels. Unfortunately, this meant I missed out on a lot of the relationship, the love, the goodness, the Kingdom, or most importantly the Person available to me. I have a sneaking suspicion it may be the same for you as well.

What I did, in the end, is what many of us do. I took the Jesus of the Bible and exchanged Him for someone, or something, far more comfortable to my way of life instead of dying to myself and taking on his Way. It simply did not work.

The saddest part is that so many like me think that this is the real Jesus and that they've begun living by the real gospel. But so often it just falls miserably short of the biblical standard of Kingdom life Jesus offers to us.

The King Sets His Own Terms

Now, it's not so much that Jesus does not save individuals. Of course, He does, and every single story of salvation really, really, REALLY matters, especially to Him. Unfortunately, in the United States, we think that everything we have is ours—like we possess it. And that means we think of Jesus like this: "He's mine!" We tend to act as if we possess ownership of the Savior rather than accept His terms for our lives in His Kingdom.

There is no place in the New Testament where Jesus invites us to come to Him on our own terms. No, we come to Jesus on the terms that He presents. And what are His terms?

Well, let's take a look at what He said:

From that time on Jesus began to preach, *"Repent, for the king-dom of heaven has come near."* (Matthew 4:7 ESV)

> *"If anyone comes to me and does not hate his own father and mother and wife and children and brothers and sisters, yes, and even his own life, he cannot be my disciple. Whoever does not bear his own cross and come after me cannot be my disciple. For which of you, desiring to build a tower, does not first sit down and count the cost, whether he has enough to complete it? Otherwise, when he has laid a foundation and is not able to finish, all who see it begin to mock him, saying, 'This man began to build and was not able to finish.' Or what king, going out to encounter another king in war, will not sit down first and deliberate whether he is able with ten thousand to meet him who comes against him with twenty thousand? And if not, while the other is yet a great way off, he sends a delegation and asks for terms of peace. So there-fore, any one of you who does not renounce all that he has cannot be my disciple."* (Luke 14:26–33 ESV)

Does renouncing everything sound like the version of Christi-anity you were sold?

You certainly give up a lot. I'll give you that, but you gain every-thing you were looking for in the first place—always, though, on *His terms*. The King of the Kingdom you wish to enter loves you more than anything. That's why He knows how much it will cost you (or how much you think it will cost you). I have found that those who pay the price are never disappointed with the exchange.

Let's be really, really, brutally clear. You don't own Jesus, and He doesn't owe you anything. Bottom line.

Now, before you go on telling yourself, *"That's not me at all! I don't think Jesus owes me one thing!"* Think about how you actually treat Jesus in real life. That will show you how you really see Him. Is He like a magic potion for the forgiveness of sins that you carry around and dip into as needed? Or maybe a handbag or wallet that, if you dip into it at the right moment (cough, cough), He can get you out of trouble or get you what you need? Or perhaps you have a wonderful morning routine that He'd better fit into or else? *"Get into my quiet time, Jesus! This is our time together."* Sound familiar?

I know that I've been there, perhaps we all have, hundreds of times. I have such a deep desire to achieve something in my time with Jesus. So often though we simply need to let go of the thought that Jesus can be manipulated to fit our plans. This made-up Jesus whom so many people carry around has a serious problem. This *"Jesus"* can't save you because Jesus, the real one, is the one who saves. The convenient Jesus whom you have in your pocket isn't real and has no power to save. We frequently move from a *"personal"* relationship with the real Jesus to a "personalized" relationship with the made-up one. Jesus is not just a nice guy who died for your sins, though that's great and wonderful. He's more than that!

If you are finding that you invited Jesus into your life and your life hasn't changed, then perhaps you find yourself in the position I was in. Maybe you're just pretending to rely on Jesus while actually relying on and even worshipping yourself. Or maybe, just maybe, there is a small chance that you may have not invited Him into your life at all. Having an encounter with the Risen One, the Living God, will certainly have a real effect. I understand everyone has a journey, but the journey to follow Jesus requires repentance and, submission to Him as King.

Now, submission to someone who died for you is entirely different from submission to some distant tyrant. Jesus offers us eternal life, right now! We can live with the Spirit of Christ in us on a daily basis. Jesus says the Father takes delight in sharing the Kingdom with us. So, when we think about submission to the will of God, we need to think in terms of His being a benevolent king who shares everything He has with us, and He even teaches us what to do with that inheritance. We should not be thinking of submission in the human sense, where in most cases in human history and personal experience the weak are taken advantage of. No, in Jesus' Kingdom, it's different. The weak (*everyone who isn't God*) are cared for and provided for in His Kingdom as they submit to the kingship of Jesus.

Far too many people say, *"Jesus, follow me,"* when the invitation from Jesus is far different. He says, *"Come, follow Me."* How do I know this?

Because I was doing life as if Jesus was an addition to my life, a parachute or a seatbelt, but He was not actually directing the daily decisions in my life. It is so much better to learn from the Master of life than it is to try and get Him to do what you are already doing. Jesus is so incredibly patient with us as we choose to follow our own counsel and seek our repentance rather than truly follow Him. Jesus is not an accessory; indeed, the life you want to live in Him cannot be carried out this way.

Who Is Jesus Anyway?

As I explained in chapter one, there was a time when I was intensely frustrated with my Christianity. I simply kept making the same mistakes and doing what seemed like the *"right"* things at the time, yet I kept slamming up against the wall. I wasn't doing what I should have been doing, which meant that I wasn't getting the results I expected from my Christianity, and I was totally frustrated by it. Perhaps you can relate. Are you frustrated with where you are at in your faith right now? Do you keep reading the Bible and what you see in your life doesn't line up with what you read in Scripture?

Well, I have some good news for you. That's how I felt, only I didn't know at the time I was headed for something great. I want you to know that you are on the edge of something awesome. Let that frustration guide you to the feet of Jesus. That's exactly what it did for me. I'd seen the gospel work in others, and I knew that Jesus was the answer, but for some reason I could not gain access to His life-giving transformation.

So, after months of struggling with the Bible, in prayer, and in conversation with people who were further along in life than me, I simply surrendered. In my heart, I said, *"Okay, Jesus, who are You really? If I am just following rules, then I can choose any religion. I feel that, if I am going to follow You, I need to stop doing it on my own terms. I need to find out who You really are, so I can follow the real You, not the one that fits into my life the way I would like You to."*

After that is when I began reading the Gospels. Instead of just reading them, I let them read me. Mostly, I was investigating who Jesus really was. I took everything He said at face value. I have to admit this was a shocking experience.

I remember taking a suggestion from a book called *Why Men Hate Going to Church.*[1] The author recommended underlining or highlighting certain things that Jesus said in the Gospels. I highlighted in blue the things Jesus said that were culturally unacceptable, straight up angry, offensive, or an all-out rebuke. I highlighted in pink the things that seemed (from my perspective) compassionate, tender, and kind. To make a long story short, there was a lot of blue. I was incredibly surprised by how much blue showed up on the red letters of the pages of my Bible.

If you read through Scripture and take what Jesus said at face value, He was actually highly offensive. I am not saying this in simply a general sense, *but I mean it personally.* I was *offended by Jesus!* This is how I knew I was dealing with a real person and the real God. If I simply agreed all the time with my god, it was likely that my god was me and not the Jesus of the Gospels.

Here's an example of what I'm talking about. Let's say someone wanted to join your church or your small group and their dad died. What would you tell them if they wanted to skip meeting that week?

You would likely say, *"Go, be with your family, and bury your fa-ther. By all means go and be there for your family. Don't worry about coming to church or small group right now."*

Yet, when I read my Bible, I'm amazed at what Jesus said. He said, *"Let the dead bury their own dead, and come, follow Me"* (Matthew 8:22).

"What? Whoa, Man, chill. The guy's dad just died. He can come find You later, right?"

The short answer is no. Jesus told the guy to come with Him right now, give up his inheritance (which was part of the process of putting his father to rest), and be with Him.

It may seem heartless, but Jesus, as always, went straight to the heart of the issue. The man who asked about first burying his father had missed what was truly first. Jesus was not illustrating that being there for and grieving with your family are wrong. What Jesus was saying was that, even in such a situation, if He were standing before you and telling you to follow Him, you'd do what He asked. Why? Because Jesus wants to be mean to you?

No, Jesus would never give this command if it weren't in the very best eternal interests of those involved. So many times, what seems like the right thing to do gets flipped on its head when we follow Jesus, and that's because He doesn't see things the way we humans usually do. Unlike us, Jesus always has eter-nity in mind.

Think of the time Jesus charged through the temple like a raging bull with a whip. He had spent an entire day thinking about it before he went back and, in an act of pre-meditated anger, ran the money changers out of the place, overturned tables, and shouted that they had turned the whole place into a den of thieves (see Matthew 21:12–17). Why was He so worked up?

The money changers had, by charging a substantial fee, kept the poor from accessing God. The poor would travel without anything to bring to the altar of sacrifice so that the sacrifice would have to be purchased when they arrived at the temple. They would have to change Roman money (with the symbol of the emperor, an idolatrous image not allowed in the temple) into the temple coin. The changers would charge a fee for the exchange. Then and only then could the people purchase a sacrifice.

So, Jesus, even in a brutal explosion of anger, was making a way for people to access God. He was overturning the tables of interest payments that limited access to the Presence. What a wonder that would have been to see!

We may feel at times like Jesus comes across as harsh on our sin and habits that weigh us down. We must remember that His anger is toward whatever is blocking our access to God. So, don't be surprised if He starts to overturn the tables of your heart.

We cannot scripturally see a Jesus who was never angry, a Jesus who was never too emotional. He doesn't think it's okay for you to have all this garbage in your life that stops Him from getting to you and you from getting to the Father. The King of the universe is not interested in cohabitation with weak little sin gods. If you want to follow Him, this Man will drive out your sin with a fury you can't imagine.

One of the most astounding parts of this story as told in Matthew was that Jesus stuck around. Normally, when you vandalize anything, not to mention the most holy site in the world, you get out, and fast! He hung around and performed miracles. Then He came back again the next day. Amazing! Finally, the Pharisees got up the courage to challenge His authority, but He caught them in their own snare.

> *Jesus entered the temple courts, and, while he was teaching, the chief priests and the elders of the people came to him. "By what authority are you doing these things?" they asked. "And who gave you this authority?" Jesus replied, "I will also ask you one question. If you answer me, I will tell you by what authority I am doing these things. John's baptism— where did it come from? Was it from heaven, or of human origin?" They discussed it among themselves and said, "If we say, 'From heaven,' he will ask, 'Then why didn't you believe him?' But if we say, 'Of human origin'—we are afraid of the people, for they all hold that John was a prophet." So they answered Jesus, "We don't know." Then he said, "Neither will I tell you by what authority I am doing these things."* (Matthew 21:23–27)

Jesus had no desire to posture Himself or prove His authority. Jesus existed outside their religious system and was doing what His Father commanded and nothing more. There was no need for Him to enter into competition with these men. They had all of heaven in front of their eyes, and all they could ask was,

"What seminary did You go to, and what pastor told You that You could do this?"

Have you ever read Matthew 23? If you haven't, go check it out. You'll find the complete awkwardness of the situation and the complete fury of Jesus. It's better than TV.

Picture the scene. It's Jerusalem leading up to the Passover, and everyone's there—the religious elite from all over the known Roman world, as well as the common people from the same. The city's full and bustling with people, with chatter of old and new friends. People are crowding the streets and catching up on their year. It's the most holy and revered religious festival of the year. Everyone's clinging to this sense of common identity while they live oppressed under a foreign government.

Jesus of Nazareth now takes a stand in an elevated place and begins to draw an enormous crowd. The chatting that normally accompanies city streets dies down, and one voice rises above the din. It's that of Jesus, rebuking the religious elite, furious and obstinate and tearing down the pillars of the society around Him—blaming them for the lack of holiness in their nation.

Here's a sample for your enjoyment from verses 13 through 15.

> *But woe to you, scribes and Pharisees, hypocrites! For you lock people out of the kingdom of heaven. For you do not go in yourselves, and when others are going in, you stop them. Woe to you, scribes and Pharisees, hypocrites! For you cross sea and land to make a single convert, and you make the new convert twice as much a child of hell as yourselves.* (NRSV)

Regular people tend to talk behind each other's back, especially when they are talking about people who could potentially ruin their lives or are greatly respected by others. Jesus writes this strategy off completely. This is an open and brutal, albeit one-sided, confrontation of an entire group of people in public. He generalizes an entire group of people who had made their whole lives about serving God and condemned them to hell with a little sarcasm for spice.

Imagine now, a very popular young preacher with a merry band of twelve men, some prostitutes out of whom He had cast demons, some rich, some poor, yet mostly young people, and another hundred or so followers of His teachings crash open the door of a pastor's conference and cut loose like Jesus did. Nobody gives Him the stage; He just takes it by raw force of personality and authority.

This is how He finishes with them in this chapter.

> *Woe to you, scribes and Pharisees, hypocrites! For you are like whitewashed tombs, which on the outside look beautiful, but inside they are full of the bones of the dead and of all kinds of filth. So you also on the outside look righteous to others, but inside you are full of hypocrisy and lawlessness.* (vv. 27–28)

I find that so many people's supposed frustration with Christianity is not actually frustration with Christianity at all. They're really frustrated with what their own ideas of Christianity are. More specifically, they're frustrated with what their own ideas about love have made Him. Jesus does not change because you feel like He should or because you have a particular philosophy about life.

If your Christianity is not working, I want to ask you a question: *Are you really following Jesus?*

Maybe the Jesus that offends you would be a better fit. Jesus does not belong to you or to your political affiliations or to your philosophy. He tells us to come and die so that you can make a covenant with Him, to the finish. Of course, He holds up His end of the bargain far better than we ever could. But the position of our hearts to accept Jesus as He is, not as we wish He would be, is a matter of life and death.

We have an opportunity to enter into the Kingdom, and He is the gate. The problem is that many people don't actually like what the gate looks like. To pass through it, you have to change, but the gate isn't changing—ever.

Something I always like to say to people we disciple is that Jesus is the narrow gate to a wide-open Kingdom. The opportunities to learn, to transform, to love, to feel, to see signs and wonder, and to know God in the Kingdom are limitless.

How, while reading the Gospels honestly, did we ever get the idea that Jesus wanted just some parts of us? Just a little bit of you and me here and there?

I had to stop for a moment, because as I was writing this, I felt the conviction of the Holy Spirit for areas of my life where I have been half-hearted with Jesus. It's so funny how we humans break ourselves into pieces to survive. We separate and hide pieces of our lives from the only one who can fix them. The irony is He knows it all anyway. Whatever is most precious to us is nothing in comparison to gaining Him and life in His Kingdom of the heavens.

Jesus is the treasure hidden in a field (see Matthew 13:44). He is the pearl of great price (see Matthew 13:45–46). Even His own metaphors seem to fall short of how great He is. What Jesus is explaining to us is that there is nothing more valuable than finding Him and keeping Him. The harshness of Jesus is always to kill the things that are killing us anyway—to tear down our man-made laws that could never get us to God. He loves us, so like a faithful friend, He wounds us. There is no need to worry, though, He's alive, and what He kills, He is faithful to redeem and resurrect. What once produced death in your life will now create life and freedom.

This is why Jesus bids us to come and die. It's not to harm us, but to make us brand new. His kindness is far beyond what we can imagine.

There are so many ideas about Jesus not based in what He actually said or did. My hope for you is that you meet *Him*, because that is the point after all, not just read about Him. We cannot just shape our lives around some new ideas. This has been tried for millennia and found wanting. I mean, the "idea" of love is not hard to sell. Of course, love is the right thing to do, but without Him, without true Love, it is impossible to find and to give in real life.

Honest Pursuit

I truly believe, if we do seek Jesus with wholehearted intention, He will be found. Oh, and when we do, giving up all we are will seem like no problem at all. It won't feel like sacrifice although it may look like that to friends, family, and loved ones. It won't feel like discipline even though those around you will think you've whipped yourself into obedience. They may see things as they will because you are obsessed. There were a million things you tried before you found Christ to fill you up; however, when you discover He is the one thing you are looking for, sacrifice will be easy. This is why He says in absolute truth, *"Those who drink of me will never be thirsty"* (John 4:14 my paraphrase).

The only way to obey Jesus is to have the abundance of the Kingdom first. Otherwise, doing what Jesus asks is incomprehensible. In other words, the only way to obey Him is to have Him.

Making the sacrifices Jesus asks for seems extraordinarily harsh when we are seeking a philosophy or teacher of regulations for salvation. Not only will you not die to yourself for Christ and for others when it's just a philosophy, you'll hate yourself and the people who don't seem to be following the rules. Christianity is truly impossible as simply a religion. It is only effective as a life-giving relationship with Jesus, the real Person.

Until we realize why He came, that He was and is real, that He did die, and that He is fully alive, nothing in Christianity makes sense. In fact, Christianity as a practiced ideology simply won't work and just turns us all into hypocrites. We know the rules but can't follow them all, so we find ways to teach the rules (which are true) without actually being able to be obedient to them ourselves.

The goal is not simply to do the right thing. It is to become the type of person who consistently acts like a follower of Jesus. That way, you aren't constantly fighting your nature in order to do the right thing. In fact, at some point, it should become hard to do the wrong thing. As Ravi Zacharias tweeted, *"Jesus did not come to make bad people good, but to make dead people alive."*2

When Jesus tells us that the way in is violent, He's not lying. Transformation, like a real labor, can be messy.

When my wife brought our two sons into the world, each labor was painful, long, and very bloody. All was forgotten when she held them in her arms, at least for the moment. All of life's regular rituals had to be relearned, for both my wife, Jessi, and me. Everything changed when the new life entered into our lives. Only something living will affect your everyday life. Only a living and real Savior will do the same for you.

But we must enter in violently—with every ounce of strength, passion, and zeal for Jesus and nothing less. But once it is in your hands, His Kingdom I mean, you will realize the things you held on to in the past that prevented you from entering fully were literal garbage in comparison.

But, again, the only Jesus that is worth having is the real one and not the comfortable one that we sometimes create in our heads. Jesus desires a relationship with you, yes, but on His terms, which are the only terms He can lay out lovingly. Our terms will always leave parts of ourselves in bondage. He, of course, does not demand His own terms simply to be in control, like you or I would. Jesus demands His terms in the deal because they are the only way to actually gain access this Kingdom life.

I think we have all been in a place before in our lives where we want a certain kind of Jesus. So, in our hearts, we set up a little shrine to a made-up Jesus who is not the one we find in the Gospels. This false sense of security, from our inaccurate ideas about Him, is dangerous. It gets in the way of our freedom and in the way of Jesus truly loving us in the way that we need to experience.

I am not saying that Jesus is all fire and brimstone, shouting from the corner that you are destined for hell (though, sometimes, He may be). What I am saying is that Jesus knows you are saved from hell, knows you are reborn in your heart, and He wants to call you out from all that's keeping you from Him.

From time to time, we all need the true Jesus who goes into a rage against the things in the temple of our hearts that stop us from being near to him. He knows that the best thing for us is to be near Him. The less there is in the way, the better it is for us and our relationship with Him.

So, just as Jesus cleared the temple, flipping tables and kicking out the money changers, He enters our hearts with the full force of His power, removing the false gods that keep us from Him.

The only question is what kind of tables have you set up in your heart that are costing you in your relationship with Him? What kind of all-knowing, completely loving God would continue to let us be apart from Him if the very best thing for us is a close relationship to Him?

The beauty of this is, if we let Jesus in, He will cleanse us with His own blood and the power of His resurrection. All we need to do is let Him do His work on our hearts.

Every time we are tempted to have a more polite and docile Jesus, we are also tempted to keep the things in our hearts that are false and produce death in our lives.

The thing that first really got me attached to Jesus, what I really obsessed over, was the fact that He never held back. Jesus was never passive about any situation that He encountered. Whether confronting the religious, demonic powers, sickness, disease, or death, He came at them each and every one head on with His entire being engaged and present. Jesus was always fully Jesus.

Imagine living a life like that. Imagine having someone in your life like that. How overwhelming and awe-inspiring and flat out intriguing it would be to live life with such a person. Think of all the times in your life when you held back when you shouldn't have, when you pumped the brakes when the right thing to do was right in front of you.

Jesus never did.

He was always fully engaged.

He never showed cowardice in confrontation.

Jesus always loved.

He never held back.

Even in His surrender, in His death and resurrection, Jesus was on the forefront, confronting the sin of all of humankind through all of history for every individual ever.

Jesus was fully human in a way that is difficult to imagine. Alive in a way that we were always meant to be. This makes our hearts scream for more, yet it terrifies us just the same. It's like an untapped power that dwells in our spirits, ready to pour itself out on the world. But we're a bit intimidated by it because we wonder what happens if we lose control. And the truth is we just might. Wouldn't you rather be fully alive, though?

Are we really capable of the same fearlessness? The same all-out attack on evil? The same hot pursuit? Can we simply be who we are in Christ to the point where perfect peace is a mode of being, no matter what is going on around us?

I'm sure you've seen glimpses of it before. Somewhere along the way, you've probably met an old salty Christian who has walked his walk and fought the good fight. There is just this *"something"* about them. They seem to possess a total peace like still water that is as terrifying as a storm.

Transformation into Christlikeness is available to anyone who would dare take the path Jesus offers. There is so much of Jesus that we simply aren't tapping into because we fear who we would become if we let Him be Him in and through us and all around us. We want to be liked, loved, respected by our peers, friends, and family. The problem with becoming a person like Jesus is that you instantly become dangerous to society. Why?

Because you're dangerous to the status quo. History is littered with men and women who followed Jesus and were killed for it.

Too many Christians chalk up their walk with God to being well-liked and respectable. But what if His way calls for something else?

To be fully alive is a dangerous thing simply because you become a threat to the world's belief systems, your friend's and family's belief systems. Followers of Jesus propose that the entire foundation that this world is built on is infected with a rot that only Jesus can cure. This requires an overturning of the way things are to be reborn into something completely new. People generally don't take kindly to others *"rocking the boat."* They like their lives, and they like their things, and in many cases they aren't willing to completely give their lives to Jesus because of their selfish desires. Jesus said, *"What good is it for someone to gain the whole world, yet forfeit their soul?"* (Mark 8:36).

Following Jesus is an all or nothing game. He pulls no punches and does not hold back. In love and zeal, He has no equal. The insanity of it is that, when we follow Him, He expects the same sellout attitude when we are filled with the Holy Spirit.

So then, what *does* Jesus ask for?

Everything. All our lives. He knows that giving bits and pieces will produce a broken and hypocritical religion. Jesus is not a handbag or a jacket you put on when the occasion suits you.

This mentality may give the impression of good religion, but it empties you of all His power. Religion simply does not work to transform lives.

Imagine a situation where you stand before a great throne. You bow and kneel, and you say wonderful things about this king seated above you. This king then offers you access to all of the kingdom, everything in it. You didn't do anything special to get such access; in fact, he invited you to come into his presence. All that you are asked to do is leave your tiny little fiefdom that is broken and falling to pieces. That's probably at least part of the reason you accepted the invitation in the first place. You say yes, but in your heart you cling to your tiny kingdom because, after all, at least it's yours. If you accept this king's offer on his terms, you'll just be a subject, a servant.

This illustrates what our problem is. We mouth the words of acceptance, but our hearts won't accept the terms Jesus lays out. *"Enter by Me,"* Jesus says, *"and only by Me, and you can have everything, all of it. You'll be part of the family. All you need is here, but there is only one King, and I am that King."*

"But wait, Jesus. I'm in charge," you say in response to His words. Your pride and sense of self-importance won't let you relinquish control. So, what do you do to make yourself feel better? What do you do to maintain some control?

You make up a Jesus who doesn't ask for everything, a Jesus who only wants a part of your kingdom, just some of your sin, just some of your *"stuff."* This Jesus makes you far more comfortable and lets you play the victim.

The real Jesus, He offers us everything and simply asks us to burn our trash, the things that won't last anyway. We just can't be in charge anymore.

Only the real Jesus, the one who can't be possessed but at the same time offers you all He has, can rule in your heart and make things right. He is the only one who can make Christianity work.

Jesus said, *"I am the way and the truth and the life. No one comes to the Father except through me"* (John 14:6).

Let me ask you to search the Scripture as you go along in this book. To accept the terms that Jesus lays out so that you may have all of Him. Yes, Jesus is patient. Yes, Jesus is kind. But remember Jesus is also severe in His love and powerful beyond our imagination. We are breathing only because He allows us to do so.

When you search throughout the pages of the Bible, find out who He really is. Finding Him and following Him will make all the difference. You will walk in the way of the violent.

THE TRINITY
OF EVIL

"Unless a man becomes the enemy of an evil, he will not even become its slave but rather its champion."

—*GK Chesterton*

I hope that as you walk through this book, your eyes are opened to where you've accepted culture and where in your life you've accepted the way of life Jesus offers. Far too often, I think we are blinded to where we've accepted culture. Jesus spoke of such blindness when He said,

> *"For judgment I have come into this world, so that the blind will see and those who see will become blind." Some Pharisees who were with him heard him say this and asked, "What? Are we blind too?" Jesus said, "If you were blind, you would not be guilty of sin; but now that you claim you can see, your guilt remains." (John 9:39–41)*

There are three gods of this earth that keep us blind, and in so doing, they keep us circling in cycles of war, famine, hunger, poverty, sickness, guilt, racism, and the like. These gods come from the root of pride. The first prideful one was the devil.

Pride, more than anything else, makes us blind, and worse, has us believing that our blindness is actually seeing.

Each of these three gods is a spirit of the earth that claims the *"God place"* in the human heart. I call them *the trinity of evil.* They are *materialism, tyranny,* and *religion.* Each of these played a crucial role in the crucifixion of Jesus, which we will get to in a moment. They all work separately at times and also intertwine to endeavor to keep us in bondage.

Materialism

Materialism makes us desire what we do not have and desire even more what others have. Greed focuses our consciousness on the world we currently live in and turns it into a world of objects to accumulate rather than a world of people to love. This is the basic premise of modern materialism. Our universities and great places of learning are defining our mode of being and our very identity in terms of a world of objects instead of a world of meaning.

On a personal level, this god makes you think that people are like objects to accumulate for your purposes, that governments are in place to give you *"things,"* and that the end always justifies the means. It robs your peace on a daily basis. It's the reason you wake up stressed about money and ungrateful for the air you breathe and the people in your life. As an example, *"From 1999 through 2014, the age-adjusted suicide rate in the United States increased 24 percent, from 10.5 to 13.0 per 100,000 population, with the pace of increase greater after 2006."[1]* And we wonder why we're depressed? Why do so many people, at a rapidly increasing rate, think life is not worth living at all?

Because we have believed the lie that the world we live in is a place simply of objects for our use. That this is the last and only possible place to find hope and true reality and meaning. That's the lie.

When these *"things"* don't do what we want or they don't fulfill our desires, we are despondent and feel disenfranchised. We begin to believe that people and the world in general owe us something. When this debt isn't paid to us, we are disgruntled and frustrated. We begin to be depressed about our circumstances. Yes, this depression is real, but it begins with greed.

Jesus clearly warned us in Luke 12:14, *"Watch out! Be on your guard against all kinds of greed; life does not consist in an abundance of possessions."*

Life, *real life,* does not consist of what belongs to you. In the end, we all die. I know you may not believe it right now, but at some point, your body will fail you, and you will pass into eternity. What you have had on the earth will not do anything for your life thereafter. Your possessions do not offer any meaning to your life now, even, but Jesus can. We need to violently resist and remove this god and replace it with the way of the Kingdom.

So, then, what is Jesus' answer to materialism?

Jesus said,

And why do you worry about clothes? See how the flowers of the field grow. They do not labor or spin. Yet I tell you that not even Solomon in all his splendor was dressed like one of these. If that is how God clothes the grass of the field, which is here today and tomorrow is thrown into the fire, will he not much more clothe you—you of little faith? So do not worry, saying, "What shall we eat?" or "What shall we drink?" or "What shall we wear?" For the pagans run after all these things, and your heavenly Father knows that you need them. But seek first his kingdom and his righteousness, and all these things will be given to you as well. Therefore do not worry about tomorrow, for tomorrow will worry about itself. Each day has enough trouble of its own. (Matthew 6:28–34)

First, Jesus told us not to worry.

But He wasn't saying this to frustrate us. Yes, this world is in our faces. Yes, the bills pile up, and the daily demands on us can drive us crazy. But Jesus gave us a clear answer to our dilemma—*"Seek first the Kingdom and his righteousness and all these things will be added."*

"Wait, like right now?"

Yes.

This, then, puts us in another quandary. *"What does that look like?"*

It almost seems like—in our Western, material world mindset—Jesus was telling us first to chase the ethereal, cloudy, confusing thing called the *Kingdom.* He was saying then everything else would pan out just fine. Many people don't even know where to start. *"How can I possibly take the things that I see on a daily basis—in fact, the things that I need—and turn them on their heads to focus on the Kingdom in real life?"* they ask. *"I need my bills paid now. I need a place to live now. I need affection and love now. I need my purpose fulfilled now. I need Ben and Jerry's now! Why should I place my hope in something that is so far off in the distance that I can hardly see its glimmer? The Kingdom, after all, really only happens when I die."*

Practically speaking, many Christians essentially feel like they need to die before they experience the Kingdom. So, of course, we place our hopes in the only things we can see. We set our hearts on the material because it is obviously and practically pointless to set our hopes on death. The fact is we are going to die anyway, and that doesn't take any kind of special person or life focus to achieve. We are all going to die, and we think, Then I will have all the things that You are talking about, Jesus. Then my relationship with You will work, my relationships with others will work, my needs for the things of this world will pass away, and I will be with You in heaven, where everything You said finally makes sense and I can use it. But for now, I just need to get by. All that Kingdom talk is frustrating.

Why is this so frustrating?

Because, in some real sense, we know that what Jesus is talking about is true. We know we've lost connection. Our hearts scream for something better, so we numb the frustration and pain with whatever we can get our hands on. We medicate and distract, even with things that seem very harmless at first. We let them take over our minds and our hearts so we don't have to think about this great frustrating and impractical hope of the gospel of the Kingdom.

"Yes, Jesus, You're right. I know You're right, but I have to ignore You for now because what You're saying just isn't practical for what I actually need today. I will get to that later, perhaps when I am dead," we say to Him.

Let me tell you a secret. Lean in close. The gospel of the Kingdom is for right now. Our materialism has blinded us to the reality that, in fact, focusing solely on what we can explain has left us destitute. Just because you can explain something does not mean it's true. Just because it's right in front of you does not mean it will fulfill your truest, deepest desires. Jesus preaches, *"Repent, for the Kingdom of heaven is at hand."* Here is a better way of saying this, *"Turn from your current way of thinking, for the Kingdom of heaven is here for you to live in on a daily basis."* The shadow is gone, and the sun has risen.

So, what holds us back from truly entering the Kingdom?

Tyranny

Tyranny can be external and is many times internal. We can all be our own little tyrants of our own lives and for the misery of those around us. If we think this is left to the realm of politics and government, we have been sorely deceived. Tyranny is any arbitrary use of power that is set in place to achieve an ideological end, the end justifies the means, so to speak. An ideology is something somebody believes that motivates their entire way of living. The way you can tell that something someone is holding to is not simply a belief but an ideology is if that person, organization, or government sees itself as having learned everything that there is to know. If you cannot ask intelligent, meaningful questions without being ostracized, abused, or simply mistreated, you are in an environment of tyranny.

Fear is the primary tool of tyrants of all kinds. We have all met them. Sometimes in the mirror and sometimes in our local or national governments. Fear, though, has been given a death blow by Christ in the resurrection.

The devil was the first tyrant. He assumed that he would take the place of God in his arrogance. Why?

Because the devil believes that life itself does not have the right to keep existing. The most extreme ideological end is his aim, death itself, and not just physical but spiritual death. Fear is simply the tool to keep people in check.

You see this clearly in people who live under oppressive regimes. The life that exists in people from the image of God is slowly eroded. Because Satan's power is limited, he will take whatever he can get until individuals or entire nations descend into chaos and death. This is why the resurrection of Jesus is the central claim of Christianity. It won't matter if the tyrant is external or the struggle is in our hearts. If death is truly dead, nothing can truly hold back those who believe. Death, being the main thing humans truly fear, has been eradicated in the work of Christ, as we shall see.

Religion

Religion is a sibling of tyranny. They are so closely related, that, at times, it is difficult to tell them apart.

Remember *why* Eve at the fruit?

It wasn't because she had some deep desire to rebel against God. It was because she and then Adam had a desire to be like God on their own effort. We took the fruit *(and still do daily)*, not because we are attempting to do something wrong, but because we desire to do the right thing, the right thing of our own choosing, that is.

Adam and Eve ate the fruit from the Tree of the Knowledge of Good and Evil, then realized they were naked, so they took fig leaves for themselves and made garments (see Genesis 3:6–7). Religion is sneaky tyranny. Even when we have a human desire to do the right thing, we do it all wrong. Why? Because we have chosen our own way, not God's.

Here is how you know you're in chains to religion. You take it upon yourself to make redemption happen. What we do not realize is the debt is so unimaginably large that all our attempts to take and put on fig leaves to hide our nakedness doesn't cover our nakedness. There is no amount of effort that can cover or pay off our sin debt.

We realize our vulnerability before God, so we make lists, rules, actions, and whole structures of power to try and reach Him. But it always ends in confusion and division among people. Like the people building the tower of Babel, we attempt to build our own lives high enough to reach the heavens (see Genesis 11). But how could a loving God allow such a frivolous attempt at righteousness?

He doesn't, and Jesus has the answer.

Personally, I have been beholden to each of these three gods, and in some ways in my life on a daily basis, I still am. But how did they affect the life, and especially the death, of Jesus? And what do they have to do with His victory in the end?

Jesus directly challenges, not only the system that oppresses (the spirit of the world), but also the men who work for it, the great antagonists of the New Testament, the Pharisees and teachers of the Law, for example. Jesus constantly picked fights with these guys. Even when it seemed they were about to leave Him alone, He went and did something like healing someone on the Sabbath, or He allowed a prostitute to wash His feet and commended her at their dinner table. Or what about when He said to a Roman, *"I have not found such great faith even in Israel"* (Luke 7:9)? It was as if He were saying, *"Your pagan oppressor that taxes you and declares Caesar a god has more faith than you, children of Abraham."* Now, that's a little surly, don't you think?

This would have infuriated these men.

Let me ask you a few questions. Do you want more money for the sake of more money? Or do you want what someone else has? Do you ever get angry, out of control, or manipulative when someone or something doesn't do what you want?

Have you ever felt that, if you attended something religious, you're a better person for it? Not because you actually treated people around you better, but because you checked a box? Think about this one.

We have all been guilty of bowing down to these three gods. What we need is a Savior.

Think about the power that these Pharisees had over the people whom they led. They controlled the temple system. They were the go-betweens with Rome and were wealthy. All of these things worked together to make many of them enemies of Jesus.

The 'Scourge' of the Religious Elite

Here's the part that is crazy. Jesus was never on His heels with the religious elite. Think about it. They controlled everything. The equivalent of the police was on their side, all the religious elite was on their side, and the Romans worked with them to manage Judea. They were firmly in control of the Jewish people of the day. To cap all this off, from the outside, they would have looked like pretty good people. They were at church every Sunday, so to speak. They kept the sabbath, they gave to the poor, and they made their sacrifices at the temple.

But Jesus didn't think too highly of this religious class. In fact, He openly and violently confronted them by healing people on the sabbath to make them furious with anger, just to stir up their jealousy and expose their hypocrisy. There is a whole chapter of Matthew (23) dedicated to dressing them down, the *"woes"* as I like to call them. Through these, Jesus shredded their sense of self-importance in the most aggressive and outspoken way possible. And He did so in public, in front of their followers, with a particular purpose—He wanted to provoke them!

Again, imagine this happening in your own church with your church's leadership team. There's Jesus tearing down everything they believe about what they have built. And He tears it down right in front of you and everyone else in the church. This isn't just some random angry blog or YouTube video. This isn't just religious infighting. This is an all-out subversion of an entire system of power and religion in public.

But *why* was Jesus so violent when it came to opposing religion? Why did He openly expose greed? Why did He hate tyranny so absolutely?

Well, let's take a look at the most famous scene of Jesus' rage in the temple. Before He turned over the tables and all of that, we read that Jesus entered into Jerusalem, had a look around, and left. Mark 11:11 says, *"Jesus entered Jerusalem and went into the temple courts. He looked around at everything, but since it was already late, he went out to Bethany with the Twelve."* Seems pretty normal, right? Last part of the day in Jerusalem, let's go see the sights kind of thing.

But what happened next? Verse 15 of the same chapter tells us, *"On reaching Jerusalem, Jesus entered the temple courts and began driving out those who were buying and selling there. He overturned tables of the money changers and the benches of those selling doves."* Jesus fashioned a whip (see John 2:15). He made one Himself. What an interesting portion of the Gospels. Jesus, who was not a herdsman or farmhand of any kind, fashioned a whip.

Imagine the disciples watching this happen the night before they were about to go into Jerusalem the next day. Everyone was talking and eating before bed, the lights started to dim, but there was Jesus in the corner, as the daylight faded, making a whip.

Perhaps the disciples were drifting off to sleep, thinking this was just a prop for one of Jesus' wonderful, practical messages. Or maybe they were thinking, *Tomorrow is going to be interesting.*

So, the next day, on the way up to the temple, Jesus was hungry. Just pause a moment here in Scripture. Jesus, the Son of Man and the Son of God, had a need. He was hungry. So, he walked up to a fig tree to eat (see Mark 11:12–14). You will recall that the leaves from a fig tree are the kind of leaves that Adam and Eve covered themselves with when they were *"naked and afraid"* as God walked through the garden in the cool of the morning. Jesus would have been there, by the way, as He is God. All that being said, the fig tree had no fruit. Jesus, not pleased, cursed the fig tree. The tree withered and died.

"Whoa, Man, it's not even the season for figs. Cool it!"

But, as we'll see, Jesus was only getting warmed up. Jesus' first move toward the Temple Mount was killing a fig tree that didn't bear fruit, that met no needs, that left Him hungry. It's like humanity's system of governing right and wrong, of religion. They all leave us feeling hungry and full of shame. But Jesus symbolically killed this tree, this idea of law and shame and making our own way to God—a way that fails in getting us to Him.

Pretty awesome start to the day so far if you were with Jesus. But that whip was still on His person, maybe hanging off His hip like Indiana Jones, or maybe hidden inside His robe. Jesus was still hungry, heading straight to the temple. When He arrived, let's just say things escalated quickly.

Let me paint the picture.

The temple was a sacred place. In fact, a sign on the wall basically said, *"If you don't believe and you enter, you will be killed."* The temple was the place where God communicated with His people, a place full of history. It was the very identity of the Jewish people.

When a festival would take place, people would come from all over to celebrate and make their sacrifices. Many could not bring herd animals from where they lived in order to make the required sacrifice. So, when they arrived at the temple, there were animals of all kinds available for sale. Not a bad idea in and of itself, but there was a catch. You couldn't technically pay for the sacrifice with a Roman coin as it had an image of Caesar on it. Therefore, you would be paying for a sacrifice with a graven image, which Jehovah was not a huge fan of (note: lots of people died in the Old Testament because of this rule).

Here was what would happen. You would walk in and change your money into temple coins. The exchange, however, would include interest. Like changing money in a foreign country, there was a fee added on top to make the exchange. All of this made logical sense in any normal context. That being said, let's get back to hungry, fig-tree cursing Jesus with a handmade whip, walking into the temple.

Jesus walked into the courtyard and started flipping the tables of the money changers and chasing people out with a whip. He was shouting at everyone present, *"My house will be a house of prayer but you have made it a den of thieves"* (Mark 11:17 my paraphrase).

Herd animals were running everywhere, money was flying all over the place, and all the while Jesus was driving out the animals and the people with a bull whip. He was at the center of a storm of His own making. Nobody stopped Him.

Imagine the absolute audacity, the command of presence, the raging intensity. Nobody touched Him.

"Whoa, Jesus. Be cooler. Be nicer. You couldn't strike up a conversation with a money changer and gently tell him he was robbing people? Why are You so mad about this but not mad at a tax collector who is blatantly robbing the Jewish people? You party with those people."

Here's why. People were being charged interest by the infrastructure of the religious elite to connect with God. To be free of their sins, to say thank you, to make an offering, to commune with God, people were paying extra in a system they had to oblige.

The common person, especially the poor person, was trapped by the system. They couldn't have a graven image on the coin in the temple, yet they had to make a sacrifice, and the only way to buy the approved sacrifice was through a corrupt temple system that had become far more like an institution of tyranny. At least the tax collectors didn't add God to their robbery.

So now, you can see Jesus flew into a rage because the people were being kept from God. This foreshadowed the way He would destroy the entire "temple model" of religion through His death and resurrection.

Jesus doesn't like it when religion stands between Him and His people. In fact, He hates it with a passion we can't fathom. It's a hatred so pure in its love for people that it can't be explained. Instead, it must be shown.

So, here is the point I want to make. Nice is not the goal of following Jesus. Kindness, of course, is important. But Jesus showed kindness in the most disturbing ways to our religious Christian sensibilities.

The way Jesus showed love was by fashioning a whip, driving people out of the temple, and condemning anyone who had anything to do with the continuation of that system. Jesus wasn't just pulling off the Band-Aid; He was out to kill the system of tyranny and religion that held people back from relationship with God.

Many of us see morality as passive. It's my definition of a nice guy. He won't engage with the world around him and is too cowardly to do the right thing. Doing the right thing would be active.

Not being able to do something is not morality. Morality is never cowardice. Staring in the face of oppression or anything that denies people true freedom in Christ is a courageous act of moral integrity.

For too long, the idea of what being a good Christian looked like was taming yourself, being nicer, and attempting to manage your sin. This, however, is not the gospel. The only way to truly eliminate doing the things that hinder you, that create death in your life, or just simply hold you back is to aim for the opposing positive. We must understand that we cannot stop doing something by stopping doing something. We cannot *"stop hating"* someone, for example. There must be an opposite and greater action and emotion in response to hatred. And the greater action and emotion in response to hatred would be forgiveness and love, respectively.

Let me give you a real-life example. My wife and I fight. Neither of us is a *"nice"* person by the normal Christian standard. It's sometimes like we took two forest fires and put them in the same house to co-exist. But there have been a few times in recent months where things just went too far. We were bordering on resentment toward one another in even the petty arguments we began to have. Add two kids (Irish twins, boys, a year and a month apart, both below the age of two). Things could, and did, escalate quickly.

So, I took a good hard look at myself in the proverbial mirror. I could not stop resenting or being frustrated and angry with my wife by simply trying to be a nicer person. That would just be a plan headed for abject failure. Instead, we sat down together and made a different plan. Rather than *"trying not to fight,"* which I knew would be inevitable because one of us is male and the other is female, we decided to purposefully encourage one another. You know what?

It worked. Three times a day, we decided to say a meaningful encouragement to one another—to actively love the ther person.

Yeah, we still fight, but now we can anchor ourselves in the reality of our love for one another. As a result, we fight more fairly, and things get far less out of hand. The point was to actively think first of the other person.

Now, imagine a different scenario where I had just tried to be nicer. What if I just gave way to every time my wife had an opinion or a desire that she deemed worthy to have a disagreement about. Sure, I could choose not to fight back. Sure, I could always just do what she wanted. But the resentment in my heart, and hers, for lack of respect for me, would grow. The chaos in our hearts would eventually bear fruit, because passively following Jesus and doing what He asked, all in the name of being nicer, certainly does not work.

Simply put, Jesus does not overturn the value systems of this world by only destroying them. He completely replaces them with the life-giving opposite. In place of tyranny is freedom, in place of religion is relationship, and in place of materialist consumerism is the concrete reality of the Kingdom.

Yes, Jesus tells us to love God and love one another. But what does He mean when He tells us to love? Jesus does not call us out of darkness and bondage to be *"nice."* He certainly was not nice all the time. Being nice wasn't His aim, but He was alive, loving, and powerful beyond what we can imagine. The solution we are looking for to live a life that Jesus promised is so far from following a new set of moral principles. And trying to observe every principle in our own strength is totally impossible. More rules, more bondage, and more religion, that never produces life.

So why did they put Jesus on a cross? Or better said, what led Him to accept the cross?

He accepted the cross because He was offering us direct access to God through Himself, which destroyed the structures of control that hold us down in this life.

Think about it. You don't need a pastor or a priest to speak to God. You don't need things to keep you happy. You don't need to be in control because you know the one who is. Every way that we find ourselves miserable in this life comes back to the fact that we make something god instead of letting God be God. For millennia, it seems humanity had no other choice. But Jesus, through His death—and resurrection life—gives us a whole new way.

People who truly know this in their hearts are extremely dangerous to the world. You have to know this. Someone who has direct access to the Creator of the universe and His love owes nothing to anybody but love. Such people now have true freedom to choose their actions, to choose correctly what love looks like in their daily lives.

You no longer owe anybody anything but the love you have been shown. But it's not a soft, constantly changing, rom-com kind of love. This love has ultimate power over the outcome of the entire universe and, perhaps more importantly, the daily lives of people.

I try to explain this kind of love in a factual kind of way. If, for example, you have a family member who is a heroin addict, the loving thing to do is try everything in your power to help them break their addiction while allowing them to choose their own way out. It is not to let them sell or steal things for drug money, or go back to their friends who are also using. This kind of passive and weak love has no power to deliver. But a good way to love this person is to sit them down, tell them that freedom is possible, and give them options to break free. You cannot truly force anyone to do anything, so that is out of the question. But a serious, brass knuckles, truth and love conversation is the kind that is needed when someone's life is on the line.

Look at how Jesus loved. He entered a world full of people addicted to one thing or another. It would not be loving for Him to gloss over hell, to tell them consuming all they can is the best way to find joy, that it will all work out in the end no matter what; and it certainly would be almost evil to give a new set of tyrannical religious principles to follow. What we need to do is become an entirely new kind of person through the life that He offers--the type of person who can do what He asks of us. As Proverbs says, even a child is known by their actions (20:11).

You see, we all act on what we actually believe. If you really believe God will provide, you find yourself becoming more generous on a daily basis, not because you have a certain amount of wealth already attained, but because you know that your heavenly Father has a limitless supply of resources and He desires to give them to you. You will stand up to large and small tyrants alike because you realize that, even if you are persecuted and hated for it, the God of the universe still does not force choices down people's throats, even if He does give the option of the Kingdom with the strongest terms possible. You will step out of a church or a religion that deems it necessary to make you earn your place before God and, where it is needed, loudly denounce such slavery.

None of these things are very nice in reality. Confrontation of the world's system of attainment and success is a dangerous game—a game that many have played well and gotten killed for. But that should tell you something. Why in the world would a group of people who are telling the world to love each other be so hotly persecuted (the most martyrs killed by far in the twentieth century)?

I would venture to say that there is an enemy in this world, spiritual yet so tangible, that is losing his grip against the violent love march of the Church of Jesus Christ. When people begin to lose their grip on controlling the actions of others, they will go to desperate measures to shut up the people spreading freedom of the kind that is only found in Christ alone, the God-Man, the quintessential Man, as Dallas Willard put it so well.

In the next three chapters, we are going to deconstruct the three "*gods*" of this world and how Jesus overturned them. I want to give as much insight as I possibly can on how you can join the revolution. These three principalities—materialism, religion, and tyranny—are in a desperate battle for control over the kingdoms of this world.

But we know who wins. It's Jesus!

> The seventh angel sounded his trumpet, and there were loud voices in heaven, which said: *"The kingdom of the world has become the kingdom of our Lord and of his Messiah, and he will reign for ever and ever."* (Revelation 11:15)

THE DEATH OF MATERIALISM

"The world says: 'You have needs—satisfy them. You have as much right as the rich and the mighty. Don't hesitate to satisfy your needs; indeed, expand your needs and demand more.' This is the worldly doctrine of today. And they believe that this is freedom. The result for the rich is isolation and suicide, for the poor, envy and murder."
—*Fyodor Dostoyevsky, The Brothers Karamazo*

Materialism is a doctrine of evil. It teaches that the only world that exists is the one you experience with your physical senses. We're not just talking about consumerism, but the whole idea of materialism. The supposed fact is what you see and experience with your physical senses is the only world you can ever know.

This is a lie.

What you see, what you can feel with your hands, what you

can taste and smell, and what you can hear with your physical ears—these are the things that the spirit of this world says, *"This is it. This is all you'll ever have."* So, we are encouraged by endless advertisement, by family and friends, and by co-workers and well-meaning slogans to live for these "things."

But we all know, deep in our hearts, what they're trying to tell us isn't true. Yet, our hearts scream for more. We are all well aware that what we see is not the end-all be-all. So, we are offered a continual banquet of consumerism to keep us occupied, to keep us numb, foggy, confused in our hearts. The heart cries, *"More, please, more. I am starving!"*

And the world responds with, *"Certainly you can have more, for only twelve payments of 299 dollars per month, your soul will be satisfied."*

We scrape and scratch and work our hands to the bone, let our souls die in meaningless circular work, to get more *"things."* The very things that we accumulate end up betraying us over and over again, losing their luster almost as soon as they are driven off the lot, as soon as the meal is done, and not even ten minutes after the package arrives on our doorstep.

We know it's not enough to satisfy our hearts, our souls, or our deepest desires, but is there another option? What is a starving person supposed to do? We must devour something, but we do not know what, so we eat what is put in front of us time and time again. Every time the purchase feels like a one-night stand, exhilarating for a moment, but an empty, cold, hungover morning soon follows. To consume and accept the present reality as it is is simply not enough.

Our hearts demand more.

Jesus knew this and offered us a solution. He said:

> *The kingdom of heaven is like treasure hidden in a field. When a man found it, he hid it again, and then in his joy went and sold all he had and bought that field. Again, the kingdom of heaven is like a merchant looking for fine pearls. When he found one of great value, he went away and sold everything he had and bought it.* (Matthew 13:44–46)

Jesus laid out a clear, unwavering solution to our dilemma of the material world in which we live. He understands that a human being is not simply made up of physical parts. There is so much more; in fact, all is available to us if we can truly see what He is trying to teach us in this parable.

The Good Life: The Abundant Life

The good life, the truly good life, is not lived for this world at all, but for another world altogether. Jesus did not present this life in a way that allows us to simply wait for death and for the next life to start. He made the astounding claim that true fulfillment can be experienced in the here and now—that this kingdom is present and available to us in our daily lives.

This Kingdom is so unbelievably good that you would be willing to completely eliminate your old way of living in order to pursue it. Doesn't everyone desire this kind of purpose? This kind of hope in a present reality that is radically different from the one that they are living now?

The answer, across all cultures, is an emphatic *yes!* This is why the teaching of Jesus is so timeless. It speaks to the human condition like no other teaching on Earth. Yes, of course, there are other ways of life, other *"religions"* that people seek to find this in, but what do they really offer? In every case but Christianity, there is a list of things *to do* in order to achieve some superior level of consciousness that will free you completely from your present reality. Jesus certainly commands us to do certain things, but how?

By becoming someone completely new with a life oriented around the Kingdom of the heavens. He does not offer us a new set of religious principles that are simply a way of achieving our materialistic dreams.

Let me say that again in a different way so we get it.

Jesus Christ is Lord of heaven and Earth, He died for all sin for all time, He rose from death, He sits enthroned in heaven as Master of all things, inferior to no one, superior to all, Lord. Not president, not CEO, not senator, not dictator. He is *Lord* of all creation. In short, you are here to serve His purposes. He did not die and rise again to serve yours.

Think of it this way: You don't want everything you ask for. I had multiple relationships before I met my wife. I asked for these women at the throne of God in my teens and twenties. Did God answer my prayer to be able to *"have"* one of these women forever? No, and I thank Him every day. Well, in fact, He did answer my prayer, but the answer was *no*, by His grace. I am sure for a number of reasons that, if those women had been doing the same, they are thanking God they aren't with me as well.

My older son is a year old at the time of this writing, and my younger son is three months old. I love them more than I could have even possibly imagined. You know what? Even in my imperfect love, I'm not willing to give my one-year-old my twelve-gauge shotgun to play with and my glass of whiskey at night. Just the same, I wouldn't be willing to give my three-month-old the food my one-year-old is eating. Why? Because they could die, be seriously injured, or get violently sick.

Why on Earth would a loving God give you something that would completely destroy you?

This is the trap of a materialistic Christianity. It turns Jesus into an unthinking genie or vending machine that can be called upon to fulfill our dreams when we don't feel like putting in the work. What kind of leader would Jesus be if He just gave us everything that suited our fancies or dreams that are temporary?

Materialism that gives birth to greed always falls short of what our hearts truly desire. What a human being needs goes far beyond our physical reality. This is why so many philosophies fall short of what Jesus teaches. The operating system that many of these teachings provide only gets you temporary results.

Jesus offers a completely new kind of life—life as it was originally intended—something eternal, right now. That's right. Something eternal, *right now.*

Imagine that you could have everything that you ever dreamed. Your life would be completely full, your checking account would have no real limits, and you could purchase everything you could ever want. But the chief limitation of this physical world would be that you were made with your spirit in mind.

So, we have this gnawing sense of hunger deep within us for something that will never fade. Why do you think plastic surgery exists? Why do you need the new iPhone? Why do you need the new car, the new clothes, the new everything?

Because deep in your heart, you know you were made for something continually new and never ending. It is simply a misplaced desire.

New things are nice. A new life is better—the eternal kind of life right now, in your heart and spirit, that burns like fire deep in your soul, in the part of you that *is you*.

Jesus shows us the way into this life. It's the reason He came. He came, not just to forgive us of our sins, but bring us into a Kingdom with wealth that goes beyond this physical reality. He came to give us life—life to the full (see John 10:10). This is real hope. This is something we can live life for.

The Thief

But Jesus warned us about a robber in John 10:10. He told us about the thief who is of the murderous kind. What have you been robbed of? What has been stolen from you, and what is killing you? You can find the answer in your own heart.

Take a moment. Take a deep breath. Think about the things in your life that were your greatest hopes or aspirations but were stolen from you. Where does this sense of loss come from? Why does it go so deep to have hope deferred, shut down, thrown away, walked upon by others? There is something here to blame, or someone for that matter. The thief.

Here's the crazy part, the thief steals from you by giving you something. For some reason we think, this time, there won't be a hook attached to this little morsel of materialism.

Ask yourself this question: Do you own your things, or do your things own you? We are made to be masters and rulers in this world full of eternal life. But too many of us are slaves to the idea that, if we could get more, we will in fact be more; but this is not the true substance of a human being.

The real core of who you are is eternal, so you require eternal things to be truly full.

Think of it this way. It's Thanksgiving, and all your family is seated at a beautiful table with an enormous amount of food in front of you. It's a meal only kings would dream of only a few hundred years ago. You eat and eat and eat until that top button needs to be undone and your body literally hurts from the food you've been devouring. As always, there are copious amounts of leftovers. Turkey sandwiches are on the menu for about a week. Now, how tempted are you to lie, cheat, steal, or hurt someone in order to get more turkey at the end of November? I know that I'm not. In fact, I am usually wondering why we ate turkey at all with so many other wonderful animals available that taste so much better.

Here's my point, and if you get this, you get the antidote to materialism.

The Antidote

When your heart is full you no longer need to cheat, steal, rob, murder, gossip, or get angry to try and fill your heart's insatiable appetite for a true, eternal, and violent love.

Every sin that I encounter with the men whom I disciple—especially the habitual sins like pornography, or gluttony, or simple video game addiction—are all based on the fact that these men want to feel *alive*. They make their desires into who they are and choose to try and fill their hearts with a baited hook. But soon, or hopefully soon by God's grace, they find themselves like fish out of water, getting prepared to be devoured by the very things they thought would satiate their hunger.

A full person is not a tempted person.

How can you tell if you're full?

You continually find yourself the giver in every situation. From the finished work of Jesus, you have received so much in the Kingdom through the infilling of the Holy Spirit and His transforming work on your heart that you cannot help but pour yourself out. This is why we end up seeing martyrs exclaim with joy that they were given the opportunity to suffer for Christ. Only a genuinely full man would be able to put any victimhood aside and count this a privilege. He realizes that, in the Kingdom, being set aside by his peers, persecuted, maligned, and even beaten or killed, there is a *joy* to be experienced.

A transformed man says, *"I have had plenty to eat, so I no longer need the scraps from your table of praise."*

All you need is Jesus. Indeed, if you come to a place where this is true in your heart, like Paul the apostle said so wonderfully, you have found the key to life. You count everything in life as rubbish, and your only desire now becomes that others would find the same table you did (see Philippians 3:8).

So, now comes the practical side of it all. How in the name of all that is holy do we actually get rid of this for good?

Start giving, and start giving aggressively.

What's the first thing that came to mind that offended you when I said that? Whatever it is, that's what has its talons in your heart. Trust me, this disease will fight to keep you sick. But it's time for you to start living the life you only imagined—a life in the Kingdom with an unlimited God and, therefore, unlimited resources.

If it's money, good. Give it away to the point that it hurts, and watch God provide.

If it's stuff, give it away. Watch the God who spoke a whole universe into being care for you.

Is it time? Give it away and watch God multiply your efforts to serve and love others.

Is it forgiveness?

Is it respect or dignity to the undignified?

Go ahead, live like the Kingdom of heaven has unlimited resources to stock up the storerooms of your heart for all eternity because, in fact, the Kingdom of heaven has that and treasures that are beyond your wildest imagination.

There is simply no limit to what Jesus can do through a transformed heart.

Is this hard?

Oh, yeah. But you didn't choose the easy path; you chose the best path. The root word of disciple is *discipline.* So, we choose to practice being people of the Kingdom—better yet—people of the King.

Jesus wasn't being metaphorical when He told us to store up treasures in heaven. So often, this becomes an ethereal reality too far away for us to grasp. But Jesus is this reality. He is the Kingdom. When we have Him, we have it all.

The simple fact is that, when we give away everything we have for the sake of Christ, then we have everything we need.

The moth and rust do not destroy what Jesus, the one who paid the debt of death, stores up for us.

This is not a partial game. This is not a game of inches. This is the way of the violent after all.

Kill materialism ruthlessly. Put it on a cross. Line it up in front of the firing squad. Strap it to the electric chair, and watch it burn.

This thief has been robbing you of your real life for far too long. Push the murderous robber off the cliff and walk away.

Following Jesus is very clearly about picking up your cross and following—putting aside self, picking up your instrument of killing that self, and following Jesus come hell or high water.

Once you have found this truth, you will desire nothing else.

Here's what you need to do before you finish this chapter. Find something in your life that is uncomfortable and offensive to give away and do it.

Whatever seems hardest, the Holy Spirit will provide everything you need to see you through.

Materialism results in greed. For if there is nothing but this world in which we live to have hope in, what other option would you have but greed?

THE DEATH OF TYRANNY

"Malo periculosam, libertatem
quam quietam servitutem."

"I prefer dangerous freedom, over
peaceful slavery."

—*Thomas Jefferson*

There is a deep desire in the human heart that reigns supreme over almost any other. It so overwhelms our beings that we don't notice it; this thing becomes us and we it. This longing has caused conflict in the home and in nations and, indeed, inside us. This is the desire to control, to be the ruler of our own lives.

A famous quote from the poem "Invictus" gives us an idea of where we feel our place is in this universe.

> *It matters not how strait the gate,*
> *How charged with punishments the scroll,*
> *I am the master of my fate:*
> *I am the captain of my soul.[1]*

Are you really? How much do you really control?

Here lies the difficulty in being our own little gods. Even when we do the right thing, sometimes the consequences to our right actions are negative reactions. More than likely, in our current culture, you will receive a violent negative reaction for doing the right thing.

Suffering for doing the right thing is just as common now as it has been for thousands of years.

How much do we actually really control? I don't mean to say that we should all give up and accept nihilism (that we can't do anything about it anyway, so give it all up). But what I am saying is that by and large, much of what happens in the world around you is completely out of your hands. Yet, these are the very things that we desire to control—and all of them!

On a larger scale, governments try to control and manipulate other governments. Rulers, presidents, kings, dictators—all kinds in one form or another in history have put the people whom they were given to serve under an iron heel, crushing them under the weight of their ability to govern their daily lives. Whether it's through taxation, physical enslavement, religion, philosophy, or creed, our history is littered with well-intentioned and poorly intentioned dictators. The worst kind is likely to be the well-intentioned tyrant because, no matter how much evil and tyranny he produces, he believes he is right, even morally so. This, then, creates an environment where there is no limit to his evil.

The twentieth century is filled with such individuals who were full of philosophies and ideas on paper that, when they took form, were horrendously evil in nature. Take two men in the 1940s, Hitler and Stalin. One took the philosophy of fascist socialism, and the other took communism. Put these philosophies into the hands of two already twisted men with tenacity and charisma. The result?

Under Hitler, the Nazi regime—based on ideological genocide—murdered six million Jews, seven million Russian civilians, and hundreds of thousands of people deemed an "anchor to the state," disabled people and the like.[2]

Under Stalin, even more people were killed. Some estimate that—with his invasions of the Eastern Block, the wiping out of middle-class farmers (which not only killed the farmers themselves but caused a severe famine), plus gulags, and people just generally disappearing—twenty to thirty million were killed (and that's low estimates).[3]

Oh, and the United States of America, the "land of the free and home of the brave" on social media, let's not forget us. Since 1973, almost fifty-seven million babies have been murdered inside their mothers' wombs or shortly after they have been "extracted."[4] Remember how ashamed the German people were for their cowardice when their Jewish neighbors, and even friends, were being removed from their homes and businesses? How they pretended like it wasn't happening? With all our desire to do good, the West has perfected the art of tyranny, denying the right to even live a life outside the womb. We don't even do this in secret, like Stalin at least attempted to. We do it in the full light of day and elect leaders that perpetuate it.

The idea of *"personal freedom."* No, the ideology of entitlement is so strong and pervasive that we sacrifice our children on the altar of this god and call it a right.

The Tyrant Inside

We are our own little tyrants, controlling, manipulating, fighting for position. In turn, our governments and states become the same, religious and secular governments alike.

Let me give you an example.

Your boss makes some arbitrary rule, or you have to fill out some pointless report, not because it's important, not because it's necessary—not because it would benefit you or anyone else in the workplace—but simply because your boss can. Your boss enforces the rules because rules are rules, because your boss desires to be in charge.

Think of a church environment where the exact same thing takes place. You're busy trying to sort out your daily life, how to love people, when you're actually angry about how you're going to pay the bill that just came in the mail, or the classic argument takes place between you and your spouse on the way to church. What do you hear when you arrive?

A list of rules on how to live a better life. *"Just do these three things for a better life! That will do it."* This is the common teaching from pulpits in America, and it's so foolish and hurtful to those without a concept of how they are a brand new person. We do more harm than good. Discipline and self-denial are not an end in themselves. This is a heresy that Paul dealt with in many of his letters. It's the heresy of the Gnostics, to be more specific. It's the old your body is evil and your spirit is good, so punish your body throughout your life to be a better Christian. No, we need transformation that comes through the work of the Holy Spirit in our self-denial. Without being born again, none of this is truly possible in the long run.

But, alas, you are still angry with your wife, and your bills aren't paid, and your sweet little children can push you right over the edge. What you actually needed was to be free of your own self-tyranny. Instead, you were given an extra load to bear with the three ways to be a "nice boy" sermon.

The first answer to being free is to let the old you die. It is less an act of doing and more an act of surrender to Christ. The idea of *"dying to self"* perhaps isn't the exact right phrasing. *"Then he said to them all: 'Whoever wants to be my disciple must deny themselves and take up their cross daily and follow me'"* (Luke 9:23). Self-denial means affirming the ways of Christ. Without following Him, you have empty discipline that will sour your heart toward your relationship with Jesus. Before we even begin to root out the tyranny and oppression around us, it must be destroyed in our own hearts. The only way, Jesus told us, is to *"deny"* ourselves. Deny is a word we don't use very often in our society. We are far more likely to *"treat ourselves,"* or say, *"I deserve this."* What does it look like to deny yourself on a personal level?

To the world in its current state, denying ourselves as Christ asks us to, will seem extreme and even insane to some. We should fast, be constantly devoted to Scripture, serve others who offend us, and love those who hate us, slander us, and wound us and those we love. The doctrine Jesus gives us of self-denial is not simply a bitter pill to swallow, but a total regeneration of the human heart. This seems like an extreme solution. But don't we face an extreme predicament? We literally live with minds that we can't trust to make decisions between right and wrong. If you need evidence of this, look at the world around you. What are the results of men ruling their own hearts? What are the results in your own life? In your immediate relationships?

The bearing of our own cross is a small price to pay for the life Jesus offers on the other side. He knew that, so that's why He was so brutally honest with us, as only love personified can be.

You know, if you shut down the noise, and really think, really look to your heart, what is it that needs to go? What is it that needs to be denied? What or who is the little demonic or habitual tyrant who needs to be dethroned and exposed for who he truly is in your heart?

This is the first step to true freedom. Take Jesus at His Word, and let the cross do its work, not so that you will die, although it may feel like death, but so that you can truly live.

We all have run from our problems for too long. We have allowed religion to be a paltry and ineffective salve for the deepest wounds in our lives. Bleeding and wounded, we walk into church on a Sunday; we walk out bleeding, wounded, and a little drunk on self-righteousness—not fully alive, but not fully dead.

"Repent for the Kingdom of heaven is now available to you."

Why would the words of a loving God be so seemingly harsh?

Because He knows better. He knows that the life you have now isn't even remotely close to what He has to offer you. He loves you with a fierceness and intensity that is unimaginable. It won't patch your wounds and leave them infected, allowed to fester and poison your life. He wants the whole package—all of you, the redeemed you and the free you.

To realize that you have been your own tyrant is indeed a hard truth to bear. But once he is identified, he has to die. It's all well and good when it's an external source to fight against, but when we realize it's our own way of living and being that has us in chains, the process is painful.

Let me encourage you. Life is far too precious to live out your days under any oppression, even if it is self-inflicted and seemingly justified. This is where the genius of Jesus is so evident, and His hatred of tyranny is so clear. It is intensely personal to Him. Jesus is relentless when it comes to setting people free of what oppresses them. Wouldn't it be refreshing if we, as His followers, operated in the same way? Could we be so bold as to say that we took the side of freedom, even if it cost us personally? Or cost us everything?

We cannot overcome the tyranny around us until we obliterate the tyranny that we carry in our own hearts. The frustration with others, even in our daily commute, is a positive sign that we suffer under this dominion. Something as simple as someone cutting us off in traffic or not moving out of the way of the door frustrates us to the point of cursing, if not in our words, then in our minds.

We are tiny little tyrants, wandering around and screaming about our rights when we are unwilling to give the same amount of personal freedom to anyone else. And we do this, not because we are so absolutely free, but because we oppress ourselves in our own thoughts.

The best way to tell what or who is in charge of your life is to take a good hard look at what really makes you angry about the people you run into on a daily basis.

Why won't you confront your boss about the arbitrary rules set in place?

Because you are a slave to the same system that he is. You want to be liked or want to be needed. *"I'm here for the paycheck. I don't need to deal with that."* Money or social wellbeing becomes the primary motivator for you, not confronting your boss, while the rule stays in place, and the whole office suffers.

In reality, the one little problem is the really big problem that plagues our society. If we allow the little things, won't we then begin to allow the big things? Don't all the little things add up to a culture where being oppressed becomes the norm?

So, let's take this down to the most personal level possible.

On a daily basis, we can choose whether or not to live under the tyranny of the heart. Don't ignore this. You can choose. Think of all the things throughout your day where you decided to stuff who you really are deep down inside and let a rule, a person, or your habits tyrannize and oppress you instead of living what is really in your heart.

Ask yourself this question about your life: Is this what Jesus intended when He died and then rose from the dead? Is this what He meant through His unparalleled teaching? He wanted you to live a life in a dull grey color, so void of life it would be unrecognizable to those who first received the Holy Spirit in the book of Acts?

Why are you settling? Why are you shutting up? Why are you letting everything just go by?

May I suggest that it is because you haven't taken the words of Jesus seriously. We think they are for later or for tomorrow. But wouldn't He want you to be free now? Wouldn't His deepest heart's desire be for you to live in intense personal freedom in Him so you can live that *life abundantly* that He so wonderfully promised?

The Solution

Jesus offers a solution for today. As we highlighted in an earlier chapter, He was killed because He was setting people free to choose the Kingdom and access God without any intermediary. Do we really understand what this means?

When a person is given direct access to an almighty God to the degree that we are called sons and daughters, it overturns the social order that is some ten-thousand-plus-years-old. If I can talk to God, and you can talk to God, then it puts us on a totally different landscape of living.

Religion can't tyrannize you, for you know the one who made humanity.

Governments can't oppress you, for even in death you choose life.

Your past can't haunt you because it's paid for.

Even your own thoughts, as evil as they sometimes can be, no longer force your hand when it comes to how you live your daily life.

This, for some, is an unfortunate place to arrive. There is nobody you are any longer beholden to, but at the same time, you no longer can play the victim. You can't shake your fist at the world and blame it for your problems when the one who lives inside you and through you has *"overcome the world."*

Sadly, many choose to live under tyranny, whether it is small or great, personal or corporate. Many continue to let others decide their fate because it seems easier. But in the end, it leads to a personal hell. The sense of self gets lost in the mire and the fog of decisions others have seemingly made for us. But all the while we chose, daily, to live under the spell of a purportedly *"orderly"* tyranny.

"It is always winter but never Christmas." If the season isn't changing, something is going wrong. The issue is that it starts with you personally.

We don't have to live in that place anymore. Jesus doesn't metaphorically set us free. He cuts our chains and our bonds in our real daily life. You can be who you are called to be in your heart. That lion that is trapped in a cage no longer has to be there anymore. Jesus has given you the keys to freedom.

> *"The Spirit of the Lord is on me, because he has anointed me to proclaim good news to the poor. He has sent me to proclaim freedom for the prisoners and recovery of sight for the blind, to set the oppressed free, to proclaim the year of the Lord's favor." Then he rolled up the scroll, gave it back to the attendant and sat down. The eyes of everyone in the synagogue were fastened on him. He began by saying to them, "Today this scripture is fulfilled in your hearing."*
> (Luke 4:18–21)

Did you catch that last part? *Today* this scripture is fulfilled in your hearing, today.

Today is the day of your salvation, if you would choose it, and continue to choose it.

It's salvation from this world's broken systems and your own broken way of choosing. Jesus offers us life in the Kingdom now. His teachings aren't just nice sayings to hear in a sermon on a weekend. They are truths to live by.

Think of all the things that Jesus taught in a wide scope. What does He offer freedom from?

Lust, control, love of money, lying, religion, anger, hatred, resentment, fear, lack of belonging—just to name a few.

Does that not sound like the treasure hidden in the field?

But here is where so many people make a mistake. They separate the teachings of the Man from the Man Himself. Jesus says, *"Today this scripture has been fulfilled in your hearing."* But how? Fulfilled in what way?

This verse in Isaiah talks about a person, a deliverer. He is the one about whom the scripture is talking. Jesus isn't ushering in a new mantra or ideology, but He is announcing Himself, and in announcing Himself, He is announcing the Kingdom. He is both the King, and in a way that is incomprehensible to the mind but fully understood in the heart, He is the Kingdom. There is no kingdom, after all, without its king.

The solution was never another tyranny of rules to stack on top of your own long list of shortcomings you already keep. It was always a *Person*. The Person of Jesus is the absolute answer to oppression in this world.

So, where do we go from here? How do we throw off the chains that bind us, open the cage, set our hearts absolutely free?

There is one great tyrant that has ruled over human beings for as long as our history has been written. Death.

Death has all the marks of a tyrant. Unavoidable, seemingly arbitrary (after all, why do we die?), it has held total power over our history for eons. It is the tyrant that has total sway even over the miserable and short lives of human tyrants.

Imagine for a second a world without the fear of death itself.

What else would there be to fear? What other tyrannies, large or small, would you tolerate in your daily life? I would venture to say far less than you allow now.

This is why Jesus rising from the dead is so absolutely vital, central, singular, in the daily life of the Christian. You are saved by the cross in order to step into a life of resurrection power. You are free from the fear of death.

> *Jesus said to her, "I am the resurrection and the life. He who believes in Me will live, even though he dies. And everyone who lives and believes in Me will never die. Do you believe this?"* (John 11:25–26)

Do *you* believe this?

If you did truly believe this so that is saturated your daily actions, what would life really look like? Would you ever truly be a slave to anyone? Even if you were oppressed and persecuted and treated poorly, if you believed that you would never die, the tyrant of all tyrants, hanging its curved blade over your head every day of your life, would be gone. What, then, does this really mean?

It means fear is eradicated in your daily walk with Jesus. What do most tyrannies use as a tool for control? Fear. Fear is dead. Eradicated. Done. Finished.

This is the greatest gift to humankind. The lack of fear of death will set you free like nothing you can possibly imagine. It's not so much that you don't make the most of every day, but you make the most of every moment because you can live to your fullest extent. Be fully alive, complete, and running in Christ to be part of the revolution He began two thousand years ago.

Jesus said it brilliantly when he baited his first disciples, *"Come, and you'll see"* (John 1:38–39 my paraphrase).

The question the disciples asked was simple, *"Where are You staying?"*

Jesus response was an enormous statement about a small thing and not just a passing phrase. We need, perhaps, to stop asking what we need to do next, and ask Jesus, *"Well, then, where are You going?"*

"Come, and you'll see."

THE DEATH OF RELIGION

"Religion today is not transforming people; rather it is being transformed by the people. It is not raising the moral level of society; it is descending to society's own level, and congratulating itself that it has scored a victory because society is smilingly accepting its surrender."

—A. W. Tozer, "The Price of Neglect"

There are a lot of terrible tyrants in this world, but the worst kind is the tyrant that means well.

At the beginning of time, when Adam and Eve committed the first sin in the garden, the enemy did not appeal to a desire to sin. The serpent appealed to their desire to do and be good, to be like God.

From that point on, we have made up our own minds about what is good and what is evil, hence the name of the tree, the *"Tree of the Knowledge of Good and Evil."* At face value, the name isn't so bad. We should know the difference between good and evil, and we should be self-conscious and enlightened and able to decide. The problem is we are terrible *"deciders."* In fact, it's incredible how often we make the wrong decision morally, yet with every intention of doing the right thing.

Think of our society today as an example. We assume *(as every great society has before)* that we are the peak of civilization, the peak of knowledge, the peak of technology, the peak of morality, the peak of tolerance, etc. Admittedly, we all know that there is work to do, that we have problems. The real foundation of the problems lies in the fact that our solutions are terrible. We keep deciding wrong.

Take abortion, for example. We think it is *morally* right and proper to follow our sexual urges with very limited restraint. This is generally agreed upon in our society. We think someone should be free to make the sexual choices that they desire. Just like anything else, there are consequences to this action that constantly go unsaid, however. One of the outcomes of sex is pregnancy. So, in now millions of cases, what is considered morally right produces an undesired result, so we have to construct a whole new kind of morality that makes abortion right. Call it personal sovereignty over the body, women's rights, or something else, but in fact, at face value, a life is actually eliminated.

Now take the LGTBQ movement. It makes your attraction to whatever sex your entire identity. The proponents of the movement themselves declare themselves *"right"* and anyone who disagrees with them *"wrong"* and *"hateful"* and *"bigoted."* I am sure many people are wrong and hateful and bigoted, but bigotry has a way of infecting those who point the finger at others for the same crime.

This desire to decide what is right and wrong for ourselves constantly falls short. Even when it started with good intentions, sometimes literally to protect people from violence like many in the homosexual community have suffered wrongfully, it begins to turn in on itself and turn into hatred for the bigot. In the end, it defeats the purpose of finding freedom and creates a new monster.

The Tree of the Knowledge of Good and Evil was rightfully inhabited by a snake. I would say in our day that it has become a hydra.

When it comes to sexual freedom, we choose to put our stamp of approval to a certain degree on how much sex people can have and with whom they can have it. In the early years of the 2000s, this was a lot. Promiscuity is generally accepted, well, at least for men. If women are promiscuous, it's still slightly shameful but extremely shameful if they are caught. This is one of the greatest hypocrisies of Hollywood and the media in general. But when lived out to its fullest, promiscuity creates a situation where women are left vulnerable to a world that allows men a free pass not to care for a child they had a part in creating. Many women are left with an option of shame or abject poverty for the life of that child. So, we make abortion *"right"* for them to choose because our ability to choose morality has objectively failed.

"Now, what does all of this have to do with religion? You chose the two most inflammatory subjects in our day and age to talk about— sex and religion."

I absolutely did because the reality is religion is exactly the same as the movements and paradigms of the beliefs mentioned above, but it is more insidious, more damning, more difficult to root out in our own hearts than anything else. Why?

Because we think we are right. I am talking to you, Christian.

What good is it to depart from the *"sins"* of our pasts and then set up a whole belief system that eradicates what Jesus was trying to do in the first place? To tear down the temple?

But Jesus does not just come to tear down a physical temple. He came to eradicate the entire model of temple religion.

There are three parts to the temple model of religion that we'll address now.[1]

Holy Men

Holy men, and it's always men, have the power over groups of adherents because they have a special relationship with whatever god it is you are trying to worship. You have to go through a holy man in order to even speak with this god. He's normally called a priest in our language, but any kind of holy man will do. The key to discovering if you are using an intermediary to get to God/god(s) is if you depend on a certain human person for the basis of your entire experience with your deity. This is called a *cult.*

Here's how I know this is real and happens within Christianity today. When my parents were young and had moved to a new city, they became a part of a small home group. The leader of that home group told them emphatically, *"You need to know Jesus through me."* What followed was over two decades of pain and confusion until God's radical deliverance from that group and leader.

If anyone tells you that you need to know Jesus through them, they are contradicting the entire reason Jesus came. Perhaps they don't say this explicitly but imply it by their actions. Pay close attention. Religion will not get you to God. It will only accrue power to a specific person. Just so we are all on the same page, and this doesn't seem like the ramblings of a child who grew up in a cult-like church, here is what Jesus has to say, *"Call nobody father, for you have one father in heaven, call nobody teacher, for you have one teacher, the Christ"* (Matthew 23:9 my paraphrase).

And Paul posed the following question, and now I'm posing it to you: *"Do you not know that your bodies are the temple of the Holy Spirit?"* (1 Corinthians 6:19–20 my paraphrase).

Holy Book

Now, the Word of God is holy, absolutely, completely, inerrant. It's the Word of God! But the Bible has been used by the Protestant movement since the Reformation as a weapon against people when it was designed as a weapon against our enemy, the devil. This means that it does convict, it does teach, it does transform, it does change our worldview, and it is unbelievably helpful and good. It means we will disagree with it and have to sort that out with the Holy Spirit, because the Bible is true.

What this does not mean is that the Bible should separate us from God. Even our sin, when repented of as the Word directs, brings us nearer to God in relationship. The Bible is a book of the relationship between God and man. It's a story of God making *"the first moves,"* as it were, to restore relationship to Himself under His perfect rule.

When the Word is keeping us from God, it has lost its purpose as His Word and becomes a dry book of religion. We are to read the Bible in relationship with God, to know what He sounds like, looks like, feels like, and moves like in our lives on a daily basis.

The Bible will make it absolutely abundantly clear where you stand with God. But there is always available a grace and love from God to do what it says.

The spirit of religion always separates us from God and puts hurdles in the way. The Word of God is not a hurdle; it is a light on our own condition and need for Him. If we choose to act upon it, we will then walk away from the knowledge of good and evil and eat from the tree of life, where Jesus died for our sins and calls us to a life of sanctification (also known as a constant transformation), and where we look more like Jesus every single day.

In the beginning was the Word, and the Word was with God, and the Word was God. He was with God in the beginning. Through him all things were made; without him nothing was made that has been made. In him was life, and that life was the light of all mankind. The light shines in the darkness, and the darkness has not overcome it. (John 1:1–5)

Take note here that the Word is a *Person*. The Word is Jesus. The Word of God is to be interacted with, not simply applied. When we interact from a place of relationship and reconciliation to God through Jesus alone, we begin to understand how much He actually loves us, how much sweeter the fruit from the tree of life actually is, and how much we constantly are in need of our Creator.

Simply put, if the Word is separating you from God, you are either interpreting it incorrectly or have chosen not to repent and enter into a relationship with Jesus. A choice in either direction forces you to set your own standards for good and evil; and whether this is a formal religion or not, you have made your own law and ignored God's plea to repent and be with Him forever, making you the type of person Jesus relentlessly confronted with so much energy: namely, the hypocrite.

It doesn't matter if you are a die-hard evangelical or an atheist or a *"none."* The bottom line is you do have a rulebook, you sometimes break it, and you sometimes ignore the things you are terrible at and embrace the things you are inherently good at.

The Holy Place

I remember growing up when they used to call church auditoriums sanctuaries. It always was a weird word for me, and I never quite understood why they didn't just use auditorium. The inherent meaning in calling a room a sanctuary is that *"God is in there and not out here."* Now, maybe that's not what is meant by it, but good intentions don't always produce good results and/or consequences. You mean one thing, but on the other hand you create a world where someone comes to the temple to appease God and seek His presence.

I am not negating the power of corporate worship.

I am not negating the power of gathering together.

I am not negating the power of celebration.

I am not negating the power of preaching.

What I am saying, is that the place honestly does not matter when it comes to the heart of worship since Jesus died on the cross, rose again, and makes us the temple of the Holy Spirit. This is both individual and corporate. If a church building is important to you to the point of idolatry, tell that to the millions of persecuted Christians around the world who are meeting in basements or in the wilderness away from prying eyes. Remember what Jesus said to the woman at the well:

> *"Woman," Jesus replied, "believe me, a time is coming when you will worship the Father neither on this mountain nor in Jerusalem. You Samaritans worship what you do not know;*

we worship what we do know, for salvation is from the Jews.
Yet a time is coming and has now come when the true wor-
shipers will worship the Father in the Spirit and in truth,
for they are the kind of worshipers the Father seeks. God is
spirit, and his worshipers must worship in the Spirit and in
truth." (John 4:21–24)

What Jesus is essentially saying is that the condition of your
heart trumps the place itself.

I want to make the obvious point here that you need a place to
actually meet. Some places certainly seem better than others, but
it is the condition of the worshipper's heart that Jesus is highlighting.

If God is with you wherever you go, what does having to go
through a set of pre-conditioned *"things"* even look like now?
What does worship look like? What does gathering with believers look like?

The place does not matter beyond giving people clear directions
to gather around Christ.

We have a saying in our church—*"People over places."* If we find
the people, the place will present itself. The place can't be first. (I
mean this as far as where God calls people to cities and regions.)

In short, in Christianity, the temple model of religion is obsolete, giving us the chance to no longer be hypocrites, to live the
life Jesus calls us to, and to make disciples who follow Him.

So, what does Jesus do with the words He says to the woman at the well regarding worship when He actually goes to the temple Himself?

Make no mistake, at this time in history, the temple is a holy place. It was the holiest site in the entire world, a place, strangely enough, where people were going to connect with His Father. But if we as individuals and as a people are supposed to be temples of the Holy Spirit, what are we supposed to do?

The next day as they were leaving Bethany, Jesus was hungry. Seeing in the distance a fig tree in leaf, he went to find out if it had any fruit. When he reached it, he found nothing but leaves, because it was not the season for figs. Then he said to the tree, *"May no one ever eat fruit from you again."* And his disciples heard him say it. On reaching Jerusalem, Jesus entered the temple courts and began driving out those who were buying and selling there. He overturned the tables of the money changers and the benches of those selling doves, and would not allow anyone to carry merchandise through the temple courts. And as he taught them, he said, *"Is it not written: 'My house will be called a house of prayer for all nations'? But you have made it 'a den of robbers.'"* (Mark 11:12–17)

Now, do you see why Jesus was hung on a cross? This directly affected the paycheck of a large group of people. It affected their ability to control people, to rule over them without serving or loving them. The men who crucified Jesus largely voted in their hearts to do so with their pocketbooks.

Jesus cursed the fig tree--the same type of tree that Adam and Eve pulled leaves from to cover themselves after the fall. Do you see the significance here? Jesus cursed the fig tree and then cleared the temple. The way of religion was weighed and found wanting to cover the sin of mankind. Yet people still tried, and do try, to hide their nakedness with a false gospel of behavior modification. Whatever religion it may be, it is not good news. It's sold to us from far too many pulpits, and it's killing us. We are still naked, we are still ashamed, and we are still stuck in the mire of our sin. So, what did Jesus do?

He killed it, and He cleared it. The fig tree bore no fruit. The temple cannot transform your life.

It's important to remember that, only forty years or so later, the general Titus tore down the temple in Jerusalem. It's almost like an exclamation point on the end of religion introduced by Jesus. Stop trying to change yourself. It will not work, ever.

It is an infuriating thing to find that the entire system that you built your life on is in fact a lie.

Imagine for years that the only car you ever saw in town was owned by the richest and most powerful man in the neighborhood. He would have one of his servants push it from behind as he turned the wheel. The paint job was immaculate and always waxed. The rich man would wave to passersby and command them to get a car just like his. Then a young upstart drives into town. That's right, drives. There are no servants pushing from behind, and a constant startling sound comes from the front portion of the device. This would bring some level of fascination, surely. How does this car move? Why doesn't it need a designated pusher? Where did he get this car? It is so obviously different than the pushed car. The young man sets up in the middle of town and offers everyone a chance to have a car just like his. He stands on the top of the hood, shouting that they are available down the road. Real freedom to drive, to leave the old town and go to the new that was so surely promised at some point by the rich man in town. All you have to do is get in his car, he'll take you to the dealership, and then he'll teach you how to drive.

The temple is a business.

A lucrative business.

Because everyone wants to get right with God.

If you own the place where they get right, and own the interpretation of the book, and are the man that makes the interpretation, what happens when someone comes and says, *"I'm God. This doesn't matter. I want to live in everyone's hearts. You can worship wherever you want, just love Me and love people. Oh, and I'm making the last sacrifice, so no one has to pay for that anymore. I'm doing it. Oh, and there is no pathway to heaven but Me, for here and now and for eternity. So, talk to Me, because I'm fixing the relationship you by no means have the power to fix yourself."*

This is a change that is intolerable to any religion, to the god of religion. Where does most persecution come from?

From the hyper-religious zealots. Muslim, Hindu, humanist, Buddhist, Christian—it doesn't matter. If you try to overturn people's protection of their god, you're going to catch some heat, even if their god is some malformed version of Jesus.

You'll know you've struck a chord with one of these gods when the religious start to lash out violently with words or physical violence. Be encouraged, you're on the right track. They are the ones who killed Jesus after all.

Why does this religious spirit lash out so violently?

Like a trapped animal or a person very broken by life, they feel they have no other power than to lash out, and it's true. Those who carry the form of religion without the power will find themselves defending systems that don't work, structures that oppress, and people who are long dead with no real power to deliver from the basic human condition.

This is why the fact that Jesus is alive is so central to genuine Christianity (the fact that I must make that distinction will tell you how far we've fallen). A living Savior who, not only comprehends, but rules the universe, and who just so happens to live inside you, does not need mindless chatter and argument to defend Himself. He is power.

If what you are doing right now has no power to save, and you find yourself defending facts instead of displaying the life of Chris, well, I'll let you draw your own conclusions.

This is the reason the gospel of the Kingdom of heaven is so absolutely volatile. If the Kingdom is everywhere and available through Jesus, there is nothing left for those who lead God's people to love, serve, and speak the word in truth and love, spreading the gospel of the King Jesus and not their own form or power structure.

If we, if you, accept the Way of Jesus, be ready to infuriate people who carry a religious spirit. The Kingdom constantly moves and dethrones the powers of this world, but they do not go willingly, of course.

The person who accepts the teachings of Jesus at face value is a revolutionary in word and deed. They're a *"power to the people"* man or woman who believes every person they come across they can love, serve, and experience the presence of God with no intermediary and no extra special steps to get there. Simple repentance and turning toward Jesus will do.

Now go, spread the good news. The Kingdom of heaven is at hand. Religion is obsolete. It has been weighed, it has been measured, and it has been found wanting. Religion is an empty void of rules and traditions that dry out the human soul and its purpose of flourishing on the earth.

But there is one catch. The only way out is the only way in: Jesus.

"Well, that's not fair," you might say.

But think of it this way. Jesus leveled the playing field. Now, anyone can enter. There is no way any of us can live up to the standards of religion. We can't even keep our own mental promises. If Jesus is the way, everyone can enter. If religion is the way, any religion, with any rules and precepts, only those that hold the power of what is good and what is evil can enter. This is unjust, not the fact that Jesus is the only way. The reality that Jesus is the only way is the fairest part of Christianity. How else would it be available to everyone?

His power, His love, His identity, and His *closeness* to us are only available through what He has already done, allowing us to become everything that we are called to be by Him, and that's a reborn human, a new kind of creation made in the image of Christ.

This is real freedom from religion—from the god that has held humanity in its grip for far too long.

End it today.

Join the way of Jesus.

Join the way of the violent.

Be a revolutionary.

Follow the way, the truth, the life.

Your heart wants to.

What's stopping you?

THE VIOLENT TAKE
IT BY FORCE

**"The frontiers of the kingdom of God
were never advanced by men and
women of caution."**
—*J. Oswald Sanders*

Have you ever walked into church and felt like something was missing? Or better yet, have you ever left church and felt like something was missing?

Think about the vitality, the life, the absolute insanity of the church in the book of Acts. Think about the things that Jesus said and did, and then His apostles did through the power of the Holy Spirit. Would you say the experience that you currently have with religion coincides with what you read?

When I began to read about who Jesus was—when I stopped reading the Gospels with the frame that was given to me—and just read them with fresh eyes, a single word kept coming to mind: *violence.*

Think of it this way. Your wife, the love of your life, and all your children are at home sleeping peacefully in their beds. You're away on a trip. All is well in your house until several men break into your home, completely overwhelm your family, kidnap them, and take them away from you.

Now imagine that you have unlimited resources. You have unlimited power and unlimited intelligence. You know who these enemies are. You know where they live. You know where your family is being kept captive and abused daily in every conceivable way. What is your next move?

I would imagine, given the circumstances, that love would dictate a brutal retaliation and retrieval—the kind of which the world has never seen. And, it's personal. This is your family.

Your love for your family at this point is not some squishy, feel good, happy-go-lucky, emotional love. Your love becomes resolve and brutal action. Your love is wrath.

Think about how personal the retribution on Christ's enemy, the devil, is. This creature stole His family. The devil has been abusing them—killing, raping, torturing, enslaving them—in every conceivable way for centuries, even the children. Christ's enemy has been raging seemingly unfazed and unrestricted in his war on life itself.

The King now comes to retrieve His family, in a rescue the likes of which have not nor will ever again be seen in history. He comes and *"on his robe and on his thigh he has this name written: KING OF KINGS AND LORD OF LORDS"* (Revelation 19:16). And *"coming out of his mouth is a sharp sword with which to strike down the nations"* (v. 15).

Now, that picture has a word that best describes it: *violence.*

Jesus does not play at the attempt of making a rescue. He doesn't pull His punches or limit His onslaught on the enemy.

And, behold, the Kingdom comes with Him.

Just read the book of Mark. No, I guess you don't even have to read it; you can just peruse it. The enemy is on the run in the book of Mark, hiding from Jesus, begging Jesus not to torture him and his minions. Sickness, disease, nature itself, and the power structures of this world shake and crumble at Jesus' words.

Jesus abolishes the entire temple system and places His home in our hearts. He wants to live in us and among us. He baptizes us with the Holy Spirit and with fire.

Do we even think of Jesus in this way as we sit in church on a Sunday? Do we remember what Jesus said in Matthew 16:18?

He said, *"I will build my church, and the gates of hell will not prevail against it."*

By the way, what do gates do?

They defend.

So, what was Jesus saying here?

The Church will attack and win. The gates of hell will not stand a chance. Isn't this what we really want?

Isn't greed, tyranny, and religion the kind of stuff that really ticks us off? All of these are inextricably linked to pride. All of these rot us from the inside out, affecting history with a wide swath of death and destruction. And death is the last enemy of God, Life Himself.

Who does Jesus decide to use to tear down these gates?

He tears down the gates for His wife—the Church.

He leaves the writhing body of this snake for His once-captured Bride to cut to pieces and turn to ash by the fire of His Holy Spirit living in her. The Church doesn't play defense. She plays offense. She does not resist. She storms forward.

What's inside the gates of hell?

More captives. More people under the tyranny of an evil that is unimaginable.

There is something so powerful here. Jesus uses those once-held captives to set the other captives free. He was the Promised One who would crush the head of the snake, and indeed He did. He was the one who would come through a woman.

Even in the midst of the curse being rendered by God, He blessed the woman with a promise. It was revenge—justice—on the enemy who had deceived her. She would not be in bondage forever. Neither would humankind be.

The irony is so thick. God uses the very death that man was cursed with to destroy the enemy and turn the tables on the devil. God uses the woman who was deceived to bring truth into the world.

Jesus appears resurrected in a garden in the cool of the morning to two women, who tell the news or bring *fruit* to a group of men.

Perhaps we should spend less time receiving at church and more time on the battlefield for the souls of men. We all truly long for it. When we sit in our pews and rows, or in our cubicle or home office, what do we really want?

What if every time you went to church you were equipped with weapons of war? What if every time you went to work you realized you were at war? What if you understood your excellence and demeanor were not that of just another employee, but an agent of the Most High God? What if you became prepared and competent and began expanding His Kingdom?

Jesus told His followers another parable. He said, *"The kingdom of heaven is like yeast that a woman took and mixed into about sixty pounds of flour until it worked all through the dough"* (Matthew 13:33). The Kingdom of heaven works itself into the fabric of our everyday lives and makes the dough rise. Your role is important, no matter what it is, because, no matter what your life entails, the Kingdom of heaven is at hand, and you are called to expand it.

How do you do this? It's all well and good that the Kingdom has arrived, but what do you do with that information?

The first step is simply being aware of where you live. You're in a whole new world now, and you have been given the secrets of the Kingdom. Use them well.

The next?

Seize it. With everything you have, seize it. If we were truly aware of what we have been offered, the value of what we have been given, we would be willing to literally sell ourselves to this new way of life. How important do the Word and prayer become? How important does that person you see in your daily commute become now?

There is a kingdom advancing, and they need to know that there is a better way.

Well how do you do that? How do I seize it?

The truth is you really know. In the depths of your heart, you know exactly what advancing the Kingdom looks like. It's to live in complete abandon to Jesus' cause or vision. When we are completely consumed by something, it works its way into the very fabric of our beings.

Truly doing this requires something a lot more like being in love or than doing our duty. Yes, duty is of utmost importance. There are things in our lives that must be done—paying bills, taking care of the kids, caring for ourselves, etc. But when we fall in love, duty is done with ease. This is why Jesus says He will give us an easy yoke (see Matthew 11:30).

When I fell in love with my wife, Jessi, nobody had to tell me what to do. I spent time with her, bought her gifts, took her out to dinner, walked ridiculously long distances at even more ridiculous hours in freezing cold temperatures in New York City because I was in love. It was the love for her that mattered; the action followed naturally.

The Gospel of the Heart

This is where the gospel of Jesus is so magnificently brilliant. It is a gospel of the heart. Jesus knew that it was the heart of humanity—the very center of our beings—that needed to be re-born. He also knew that, if we really got to know who He is, we would have access to the Kingdom because, in a way that is inexplicable but easily understood in our hearts, Jesus is the Kingdom.

Did you catch that?

If we get to know Him, we enter in.

The Kingdom of the heavens is not a kingdom of principles but of a Person—a God who fills the universe that He has made and makes Himself humbly available to have relationship with His created people. And He does so, not begrudgingly or half-heart-edly, but with everything that He has to offer. He even goes so far as to call us co-heirs of everything that he has (see Romans 8:17). *That is some good news!*

You are not just saved; you are redeemed, given a new place in this suffering world as a member of the family. We draw near to Jesus, and He draws near to us. To truly be alive in the King-dom, we must become alive in Him, alive to Him, and aware of all that He is doing. For this, He gives us the gift of the Holy Spirit, who will always tell us what is on the heart of God. More often than not, it's people. People are the point. The expansion of the Kingdom happens in the hearts of people whom God wants to bring home.

Yes, of course your sins are forgiven, but there is so much more! Please do not sell yourself short. The slate is not only wiped clean, it is filled with a banquet of goodness beyond imagination. You are returned to your natural state like a plant once withering in a pot is returned to its proper place in the wild where it can spread its roots and grow unhindered under the care of its Creator.

He's alive.

Come on, are you seeing this? The enemy is outmatched, out-flanked, and out-strategized. The devil is fooled and beguiled by the King of kings. A man, the second Adam, gives this gift of *life* back to humanity.

Soon, eleven terrified men behind a locked door will be set on fire and, in turn, set the whole world on fire. That is your heritage—the men who *"turned the world upside down"* (Acts 17:6 ESV).

This isn't some passive mission of emotional love. It was planned, calculated, brutal, and executed flawlessly. The war still rages, and Jesus invites us to join Him in victory, becoming ones who triumph over the enemy *"by the blood of the Lamb and by the word of their testimony"* (Revelation 12:11).

Be careful, though. This kind of love will change you. In fact, it will transform you. It's not a weak emotional kind of love that's spewed all over social media. Christ's love for you and the Church is eternal, unwavering, without rival, supreme, for our *"God is a consuming fire"* (Deuteronomy 4:24).

HOW TO DIE SO YOU CAN LIVE

"Lazarus! Come forth!"
—*Jesus of Nazareth*

There are things in our lives that are dead. They literally stink of death. You know exactly what I mean. Usually, these consist of the actions, words, or thoughts that make us realize how weak or how sinful we actually are. And these produce death in our lives.

The good news is you don't have to keep them. You can let them really die. It is funny how the things in our lives that produce death tend to take on a life of their own; paradox is so much fun!

Think of it like this: Death is not a thing. It is an absence. Darkness would not exist except for the fact that there is light. Death would not exist except for the fact that there is life. Death is the absence of life.

The things we do, say, think, feel, and believe that are out of alignment with who Jesus is produce death in our lives. Because life itself, the logos, the Word, the one who spoke life into being and *is life* Himself, who defeated death, is not present in those thoughts and actions.

Think of it this way. Jesus' death stepped into the void and filled it with life through His resurrection so that those who believe in Him won't die.

> *Jesus said to her, "I am the resurrection and the life. The one who believes in me will live, even though they die; and whoever lives by believing in me will never die. Do you believe this?"* (John 11:25–26)

So, what do we do?

We let Him in, and He turns on the light of *Life.*

So, what does it mean then to die with Christ?

If we can figure that part out, then we can step into resurrection life in Him. Both of these phrases are wonderful and poetic and beautiful, but how do we do them? I think you'll find that you already have the answer. It's just not easy to do.

What does Jesus really mean when He asks us to pick up our cross and follow Him? What does He mean when He tells us to deny our own life to be His disciple?

Jesus said,

> *If anyone comes to me and does not hate his own father and mother and wife and children and brothers and sisters, yes, and even his own life, he cannot be my disciple.* (Luke 14:26)

I am going to assume that when you are reading this you are physically alive and that you hope, like most people, to live a long and fulfilling life. Although martyrdom is something that we must be willing to face if indeed the time does come, most Western Christians will be socially ostracized at worst. Death to self, to the point of hating your own life to follow Jesus, seems like something difficult to grasp in our daily walks with Jesus.

In the famous Luke 14 passage, Jesus said a few things about the cost of discipleship that are difficult to swallow. He told us to carry our cross, to hate everything in comparison to Him (including our own lives), to count the cost, and to be salt with flavor *(because salt without flavor ruins even the manure pile)*.

It is clear that following Jesus is to be taken seriously, and the way you may be currently living your life might not cut it. He urges us to take into account what it will truly cost us before we choose to become His disciple.

Picture your life like a tree with hundreds of branches that grow out from it. Those branches produce different things, either life or death. The branches that are dry and rotten produce nothing and rob your tree or life of its resources. The branches that are alive and good produce fruit that enriches your life and the lives of those around you. Now imagine that Jesus comes along, takes one look at your life and says, *"The whole tree needs to come down, and we need to start from the beginning."*

All that work, all your strategies and efforts to make life what you want it to be, has to be cut down and burned so the new life can take root and grow. Why would He want to take down the whole thing?

Because the reason part of your life is producing *"death"* is that the core of the tree has a disease. This sickness starts with sin and eventually infects the whole tree. So even when we think we are doing the right thing, the fruit that we are producing is coming from a place of self-directed effort. The attempt we make is the same attempt Adam and Eve made: We decide what is good and right for ourselves apart from a relationship with God.

This is why the cross is so difficult to bear that Jesus asks us to carry, and why, in the end, it sets us free. The problem was never just the *"things we do."* It was truly who we were before Christ. Even the good things can spring up from a motive of self. Jesus said it was hard for a rich man to enter the Kingdom of heaven (see Mark 10:25). Why? Everything is looking pretty good. You've grown a good tree, so why cut it down?

There is only one way to the life and the life more abundant that Jesus talked about. It's complete and utter surrender. This literally means you are putting your life in the hands of another, the hands of Jesus, and saying, *"Do what You will, not what I will."*

Why is this so hard?

It means admitting we are wrong and doing so daily at times.

Think of every stupid argument you have ever had with yourself or with others, where you eventually had to admit you were wrong or, in fact, never did. Things would be a lot simpler if someone would just stop and say, *"You know what? I was wrong, and I am sorry."* But this rarely actually takes place.

What Jesus is effectively telling us is we are so wrong in the way we approach life that we don't even know it's wrong, so we need to start over. Luckily, He shows us the way.

Jesus' Way

I think the best place to start on learning how to live our lives out in this way is to look directly at the life of Jesus. What did He show us?

Jesus allowed Himself to be killed. It's a mistake to think that Jesus was surprised by the events that led up to the cross and was *"caught"* and then sentenced to death unexpectedly. Basically, it's incorrect to think He did it all against His will. Every single fiber of the life of Jesus was laid down in surrender to the will of His Father.

A simple way to approach this is to think of the thing or part of you that you fear losing the most. Hold that thing in your mind. This is precisely what Jesus is asking for.

In one way or another, we all fear death. We are all survivalists, and our survival instinct is one of the deepest, if not the deepest, physical instinct we have. We think that, if we can hold on to a few trinkets here and there, we will be able to cheat death in one way or another. The reality is we will all die. So, what if there was a way that we didn't have to fear death at all? The reason so many devout followers of Jesus stared death in the face with peace and even joy in their hearts is that they had already experienced it thousands of times before their actual physical bodies were in danger of dying. They had already practiced dying, and this was just another way.

What can we do to practice like the great saints who came before us? How can we on a daily basis carry our cross?

The key to doing anything our minds and hearts are accustomed to is to aim for something altogether different than we might think. For example, let's say you're trying to break an addiction to porn. At least two-thirds of all men, around 67 percent of all men, admit to watching porn at least once a month. Christian average? About the same. We know porn is bad. It degrades women, ruins relationships, and literally destroys our creative capacity psychologically, not to mention the far-reaching societal effects that *"trickle down"* from this. What can someone do who is addicted to something?

Likely, they've already tried *"stopping."* You cannot stop an addiction by simply attempting to stop. Something altogether different must be done. When we put something down, something must be picked up to replace it. Jesus offers us the solution, our cross. So, how do we practically do this on a daily basis?

Say a temptation to watch porn rises up in you, as it may be now since the word itself is a trigger for some. Keep reading. What is the simplest and most effective way at the moment to pick up your cross and follow Jesus, to be His disciple practically in the moment you are in?

First things first, invite Jesus into this and tell the truth. Jesus is alive. His Spirit lives in you. It's easy in moments where we must choose the right thing to want to place Jesus at a distance, but

He picked up His cross in order for that to no longer be the case. Remember to whom you have access.

Second, give that desire to Jesus with your words. Give it away. The temptation does have a way out. Be extremely, brutally, clear with your words.

Third, find your replacement. If its intimacy you lack, for instance (in many cases you are seeking a false intimacy in this case), aim for something higher now than just quitting this addiction. Aim for loving your wife with a text or a call, for going outside to pray for those you love, for going to the gym to care for your body, for writing out your plan for the next day to achieve your goals, for reaching out to a friend you haven't spoken to in a while, for writing thank you cards to those who have influenced you. Have a list of replacements just in case some fall through.

The overall concept here is that dying to yourself means preferring others above yourself. It's not self-abasement or *"I am just a worm"* mentality. No way, you're more than a conqueror in Christ Jesus, you are a son of the Most High God, the Ruler of the universe. You are washed in the blood, dead to sin, but alive in Christ. Remind yourself of that. When you realize how unbelievably rich you are in Christ, you realize that you can afford to give any kindness to others. Of course, this is easier said than done, and it takes practice and the grace of God to empower us to pick up that cross and die so we can be reborn in Christ.

"Death Ground"

There is a tactic in the classic book *Art of War* by Sun Tzu called *death ground.*[1] The principle is that, when you are attacked by a much larger army, you place the men at your command on death ground, preferably with a river or mountain range at their back, so retreat is not an option. Men can overcome overwhelming odds when they feel they are already dead.[1]

I remember coming back from a particular trip where I had failed when it came to lust. I confessed to my wife far too late but eventually was honest and told her I had watched porn. After her initial justifiable anger, she forgave me. Then she said something I'll never forget. *"You need to treat this like a war, the only way you can win is if you know that you are in a fight. The only right mentality with this is all out war."* This is good advice and has saved me so much grief by learning to be on the offense when it comes to sin.

The best way to approach any sin that entangles us is in a mindset of war. The enemy hates you. He hates your friends. He hates your family. He hates all things good. He wants you to doubt what Christ has done for and in you so that Christ can't do something with you. Why do you think that is?

Because a free man in Christ is a terror to the devil. A dead man with nothing to lose, because he has already lost his life to Christ, is what the devil fears the most. He fears you. He fears your talent. He fears your being wholehearted. He fears the Holy Spirit's breaking out of you to expand the Kingdom of the heavens around you. You are feared.

The enemy of your soul knows that a man or woman fully alive cannot be reasoned with. This is why, when he sees the Lion inside you, his favorite tactic is to distract you and keep you in a lull of half-hearted living.

Think of a lion in the circus. What do the ringmasters do to keep the lion from ripping their heads off?

Distraction.

I want you, by the time you finish this book, to get the taste of blood in your mouth. I want you to realize that God made you in order *"to live a life worthy of the calling you have received"* (Ephesians 4:1).

When you realize that you are already dead, it does not enter into your mind to simply give up. Realize that on the other side of death is ultimate glory in Christ. Live a resurrected life in Him.

You see, the best soldier is the soldier who is already dead.

Feeling angry about a slight to your pride? Or is someone in your way? Feeling lonely and maybe the bottle would make you feel better? Got some time alone and the idea of porn sounds like a good release? Starting to fantasize about harming someone who hurt you? Or are you depressed about a relationship that you don't yet have? Are you continually working late and avoiding coming home to your spouse or family?

Now, is that how a dead man acts?

Of course not, those parts of him have been burned by a process of drawing close to Christ on a daily basis through setting aside time for solitude, silence, study, fasting, communion, celebration, prayer, you name it. Pick a spiritual discipline to practice so, when real temptation comes, you're ready to swing away at the enemy and take ground instead of losing it. Let the great Teacher be your coach in this life. This is the life of a disciple, continually dying so that you can really live.

The old branches weren't working. The tree had a disease, so you surrendered to Jesus so He could cut it down. Now, a new tree is growing out of the scorched ground, the nutrients themselves provided by the old, dead you. Never allow the enemy to fool you into thinking that you are the scorched soil you see. Let it be a reminder that the old you has died and Jesus has turned your sin into His glory by dying for you.

You are a new creation in Christ Jesus.

I remember I was sitting early in the morning journaling and listening to God. For almost a full year, I was in a deep identity crisis. I asked Jesus what I should do about this. He told me a story, as He so often does. Here it is.

A lion was walking through the savannah. Young, virile, and full of strength that his Creator had given him. He often did what came naturally to him and hunted game so that he could eat. On one particular successful hunt, as the lion was eating his prey, an elephant wandered by and noticed what he saw to be a ghastly scene—the lion's mane wet with blood and a family of lions around him devouring the prey he had provided. The elephant trumpeted and shouted at the lion, using the incomprehensible words only animals use, saying, "You should not do this. What you are doing is wrong, and you should no longer hunt. Look at the blood! Look at how you're leading your family! Look at the chaos and mess you have created!" The lion on that particular day was cut to the heart. He asked the elephant (who of course is an impressive creature so even the lion was impressed)

"What should I do?"

"Follow me, and enjoy the grass and fruit with me. Put away your life of violence."

So, for a time the lion followed the elephant, as much as he couldn't chew it and his stomach turned with pain, the lion tried as he may to eat what the elephant ate and live like the elephant lived. Over time, though, he began to lose his strength, his ribs began to show, and his family looked the same. But he continued, trying to learn from the antelope and the wildebeest as well. Perhaps what they ate would fill his belly. Unfortunately for him, he became weaker still.

Perhaps by chance, and perhaps not, he was one day at the watering hole surrounded by animals who no longer feared him as a threat. He saw his reflection and groaned in his heart at what he saw. A gaunt face, a matted mane, a former lion. He looked across the water and saw the other animals begin to panic and scatter. A great lion, larger than he had ever seen, was walking calmly to drink his water at this same hole. The great lion looked the former lion in the eye, and without words bid him, "Come, follow me, and I will show you again, and more, of who you are."

At that moment, he knew he was choosing between life and death, not just for him but for those he was responsible for, the entire pride. He knew there would be a cost to be a lion, the mess, the blood, the fear that others may feel at his presence, but he knew now that he could be nothing but what he was.

Know that the life you are called to live is not one of passive grazing. You are called—no—you are even made to live a life of danger and to be dangerous to your enemy. This is why the enemy fears you. This is why he distracts you. I almost take pity on the devil himself if you meet the great Lion and begin to follow Him, for He will kill the old grass-eating, passive you, and show you how to hunt.

If you die, you can live.

LIONS IN THE CHURCH

"Lord, save us from off-handed,
flabby cheeked, brittle-boned, weak-
kneed, thin-skinned, pliable, plastic,
spineless, effeminate, ossified, three-
karat Christianity."
—*Billy Sunday*

The vast majority of churches currently fear forceful men in attendance. An easy way to be sure of this is to ask yourself the question, *"Would Jesus be welcome in my church?"* This may seem heretical, even downright anti-church, but it's not. Let me be abundantly clear, I love the Body of Christ, I love His Bride, and this is why this chapter is so important to me and, I believe, to the modern Western church. Jesus was, indeed, a man. To ignore this and to ignore the qualities of manhood that are in His personality is to set Him aside altogether. Let's take a quick look at the plight of men in general, then we can move on to how this is affecting the church.

In general, men take the dangerous jobs in our society. From 2003 to 2018, men accounted for 92.5 percent of workplace deaths.[1] This is the way things have been for millennia. Men do the war fighting, the logging, the hunting of big game, etc. This takes a certain level of willingness to face danger in order to provide and protect family and the societies those families reside within. This is also the reason so many of the things we rely on on a daily basis actually work. Our phones, our houses, and our electrical grid stay functioning because men by and large are willing to face the danger necessary to get these jobs done.

For the most part, men have faced danger for millennia in order to provide for their families, protect those they care for, and to explore, pioneer, and generate wealth. These are also the kind of men who have, over the last two thousand years expanded the reach of the Church—going to places where they will likely be killed, tortured, and imprisoned for the sake of the gospel. But something has changed.

There is something you will notice today in daily Christian life in the West. It is completely safe. People come with an expectation of general safety. We don't ask too much, and we wonder why the gospel doesn't reach our neighbors. When the comfort of the gospel takes precedence over the sacrifice and danger of the gospel, we end up with impotent churches, unable to reproduce disciples effectively and bring transformational power to their communities.

Why?

I would suggest it is a lack of men willing to be courageous in bringing the gospel to the darkest places in our cities.

This isn't all their fault, though. Think about an ordinary church service. Would you say that is the type of thing a man wants to spend his Sunday doing? We walk into a building with anywhere from a hundred to a few thousand people, most of whom we know on a surface level. We must be good at small talk, to start, not be to verbose or direct in our approach. As we walk into the service, we are greeted with worship or singing. It's difficult for me to imagine taking a man off the lumber line, or a Wall Street trading floor, and throwing him into a worship service, all the while expecting him to feel like he has a place in the church.

We sing, then sit, then are asked to give, are told a few announcements, then sit for thirty minutes to an hour to listen. But where do we engage with what Jesus actually asks us to do? Where is the tangible hands-on gospel?

Typically, men have a hard time grasping church because they have a hard time seeing what it's for—especially the men who would be the risk-takers of the faith. Where, in your church, can they take a risk? Besides being asked to be *"vulnerable"* with other men who haven't proven themselves in the battle of daily life together?

We need lions in the church.

I had a vision one Sunday in church. I saw lions in the city I lived in dragging game into the church. The chairs flew everywhere, there was blood on the ground, and the game they brought in was laid about on the floor. It was a total mess and seemed like complete chaos—hairs flying everywhere, the rows were scattered, and all semblance of a *"church service"* was out the window. The attendees were completely aghast and offended, but mostly afraid as they thought, *Why such a huge mess? What did these animals think they were doing to our service? Are they going to come after us as well?*

I asked Jesus what was meant by this vision. He made it clear to me that lions were missing in the Church. That, in fact, part of who He is was dramatically unrepresented in the Church. To be fair, this was a time in my life when I was searching for answers on how to follow the Jesus I had been unknowingly presented. This was the kindly, soft, Jesus nice in every way, but then I read the Gospels and was constantly amazed by what Jesus had to say and what He did. I read Revelation and became even more amazed at the stark reality of the Lion of Judah—with a tattoo on His thigh and swords leaping out of His mouth, devastating His enemies. I feared Him, yet I adored Him. I wanted to be like this Man who was and is so unashamedly honest, so absolutely true, and who is to be feared

This was a Jesus who I could follow. It was the fact that He was so powerful that made His mercy and grace so unbelievable in all the right ways.

We have missed the reality of Jesus as the Lion of Judah, and as a result, our churches are emaciated and struggling to find purpose. He cannot be the Lamb unless He is the Lion. We cannot have the parts of Jesus that bring us comfort without the parts of

Him that confront us.

In the same way, we cannot have the comfort the Church of Jesus Christ brings to the lost without confronting what ails them in the first place. This is where I believe we must open the doors of relationship to men who make us uncomfortable, who do not fit the norm. This, of course, is a double-edged sword. Dangerous men can, of course, be just that, dangerous to those around them. Men who are dangerous and following Jesus will become a force that can transform the world.

Take the central figures of the Bible. Abraham destroyed a whole army to rescue his nephew and family. Samson killed hundreds of men with the jawbone of a donkey. David established the kingdom of Israel with the edge of the sword. Peter was beaten severely for Jesus and rejoiced in the privilege. Paul the apostle was converted in the middle of going to destroy the church and went on to establish the very thing he set out to destroy— and with the same tenacity. These men were lions of their day. Dangerous men, to be sure. Men who *(for the most part, with some serious repentance needed at times)* followed God with all their hearts.

Do we have room for men like these? Can what we have set up as church allow for this kind of insane, risk-taking personality? What we must keep in mind is that, if we truly decide to follow Jesus, we will become dangerous people, but in all the right ways.

And, yes, this will make a mess.

The most poignant portion of my vision was the fact that these lions made a mess. We have to be prepared for these types of people to *"blow up"* some of the things that we are used to but don't really matter and to shake the foundations of our religious bias as they lead and advance the Kingdom. This is a scary proposition for most of us, but it has time and again been shown in the Word of God that God consistently honors risk based on His promises.

The largest struggle that we have with these type of people is our inability to control them. This does *not* mean that they cannot be led. But those who follow the way of the violent have shrugged off and been freed from the chains of tyranny and will not easily let them be placed on themselves or those whom they love again.

We must remember what Proverbs 14:4 says, *"Where there are no oxen, the manger is empty, but from the strength of an ox come abundant harvests."* And we can only imagine what mess lions make!

Think of the scene again where Jesus cleansed the temple. Tables, coins, cattle, and people were scattered all over the place. We have to think what was left in the wake of what He did. Jesus was furious because access to God had been blocked by a tyrannical religious system--a system He eventually shattered with a loving sacrifice, a messy, seemingly over the top sacrifice. Why choose a time in history where you would die in the most brutal fashion possible anyway?

Jesus knew that he was unsettling to the religious elite and that

His followers would be as well. Systems like this don't get over-turned without a mess.

Our path on the way Jesus lays out for us involves risk but even greater reward.

The type of people whom we need to enliven and revive church are many times not commonly welcomed there. They are seen too young, too old, too irreligious, too raw, too unformed.

They are men, plain and simple, the type that Jesus found and called to follow Him when He walked the earth. They do not look the part, they offend society, they are many times too rash, but perhaps that is exactly what He's looking for, and not just two thousand years ago on the shores of Galilee, but right here and right now in our day and age. Put a man like this in the hands of Christ, and the world will shake at the transformation.

V. HOW JESUS TEACHES THE WAY

"What good is it for someone to gain the whole world, yet forfeit their soul?"

—*Jesus of Nazareth*

Jesus is the point.

Of all the great principles and teachings in the world, the great religions, no ask is as great in every way as what Jesus asks of His disciples. At the same time, what He has to offer us has no equal. From the first disciples all the way to you, Jesus offers this, *"Come, and follow Me."*

Follow Him where? How? And, most importantly, why?

Why is history littered with people who have lived for Jesus and died for Him?

Because you can get no further than Jesus. Indeed, history itself finds it impossible to move on from Him. Even in circles that do not believe in God, His teaching and His life are a constant stumbling block to those who would try and move past Him. Yes, you can try, but nobody has stood the test of time in truth, in teaching, in power, in sacrifice. To add to all this and justify and prove everything that He did, Jesus came back from the dead.

The real problem that we face as Christians and even those who are beginning to become interested in the teaching and life of Jesus is His all-too-direct statements that He is God, and He bids you to come and follow Him. We may attend church for years, perhaps even decades, and still struggle to figure out what to do with these audacious claims that Jesus makes. It's good to wrestle with these, to even hold them up to scrutiny, but at some point a decision must be made. He cannot be just another good man who tells us another way to improve our lives. Jesus does not claim to be one among many moral teachers; He claims directly that He is God and that following Him is the only way to God.

Here is the beautiful thing about all of this, Jesus clearly shows us in His teaching, power, sacrifice, and resurrection how to follow Him. We may sit in a row for an hour or two on a Sunday, but the life of Christ in all its glory shows us how to live on Monday when we wake up. When the real concerns of life confront us, when an argument with our spouse won't end, when we have a child that refuses to act correctly—or when our jobs, or friends, family, and even our bodies fail us--His teachings remain true. They are true, not only in the reality that what He says is true, but true in the sense that they are tested and worthy of practicing. Like a chair supports your weight or the roof of a house keeps out the rain, His teachings remain perfect and able to support and hold up a life worth living.

So, what must we do to step out from our casual approach to what Jesus says, feeling almost hopeless in how grandiose the ask is, into doing what Jesus commands? How do we respond to the call that the disciples received?

> *As Jesus was walking beside the Sea of Galilee, he saw two brothers, Simon called Peter and his brother Andrew. They were casting a net into the lake, for they were fishermen. "Come, follow me," Jesus said, "and I will send you out to fish for people." At once they left their nets and followed him.* (Matthew 4:18–20)

Imagine for a moment you are one of these men and you're going about your regular daily work, sitting at a desk or digging a ditch, sweating and stressing about your mundane daily life. Suddenly, an enigmatic teacher happens to walk by. You've heard Him teach in church on Sunday, and you've heard some of the radical new things that He has to say. Perhaps for weeks or months you've been intrigued, had dinner table conversations about Him, measured what He has to say in your late-night conversations with friends. Now, what if He asked you to come with Him? To travel with Him, leave your job, your regular life, your safety net?

Maybe it would be a welcome relief, a new adventure. Maybe not so much. How can this call to follow be trusted?

For the most part, when we first decide to follow Jesus, we have no real idea what we are getting into. Remember it is later on when Jesus asks His disciples to take up their cross and follow Him, to eat His flesh and drink His blood; but something about

Him told them that He was worth following. The fact that He could say the things that He said to these men and they still continued to follow is incredible in and of itself. Why could they follow Him?

Because they believed him.

Why must it be Him and Him alone?

Because it could not be any other way. The greatest possible sacrifice is the only way into this family. It's a sacrifice and life that cannot be surpassed.

Why did men drop their nets and leave their jobs and families, all sense of stability in their lives, to follow Him?

Because they saw Him and they knew Him. We must do the same.

It is so unfortunate that so many jump into following Jesus with such blind faith, for faith is not blind at all, but sees absolutely clearly—perhaps clearer than the words you can see on this page right now.

> *"Suppose one of you wants to build a tower. Won't you first sit down and estimate the cost to see if you have enough money to complete it? For if you lay the foundation and are not able to finish it, everyone who sees it will ridicule you, saying, 'This person began to build and wasn't able to finish.' Or suppose a king is about to go to war against another king. Won't he first sit down and consider whether he is able with ten thousand men to oppose the one coming against him with*

twenty thousand? If he is not able, he will send a delegation while the other is still a long way off and will ask for terms of peace. In the same way, those of you who do not give up everything you have cannot be my disciples. Salt is good, but if it loses its saltiness, how can it be made salty again?"
(Luke 14:28–34)

What is the price? Everything. What do you gain? Far more than you could give in a thousand lifetimes. In giving up what you think is your all, you find that it wasn't the sum of your life at all. It was a paltry attempt at what Jesus offers us freely. The Kingdom of the heavens becomes available in every facet of life to those who would choose to die and gain everything.

Faith knows the cost very well. When we step into discipleship with Jesus, we should know the same: that it will cost.

What is it worth, though?

Every human being makes decisions based on faith, every single day. You sit in a chair because you believe it will hold you. We turn on the tap, knowing water will come out. We turn the key of our ignitions (some may need more faith than others), knowing that our cars will start. All by faith. This isn't blind decision making. We may not understand the physics of a chair, or be an expert plumber, or an auto mechanic, but we know the things that work in our daily lives just simply work. By daily experience, we see the very basic things that we have faith in provide for our needs.

What did the early disciples see in Jesus, and what can we see, that would provide us with enough *"pay off"* to follow Jesus into the death of self and rebirth that He calls us into?

Love, relationship, and a new reality.

Knowing Jesus

The disciples believed that what Jesus said was true, not because His words were simply inspiring or because He could draw a crowd. They continued to follow because they knew the Man. They knew that He didn't just tell the truth but that He was the Truth. He was True-ness Himself.

The only real way to follow Jesus is first to get to know the Man Himself.

There are a lot of Christians who know about Jesus. In fact, they know perhaps too much about Jesus, but they do not know Him at all. To experience the Man Jesus Christ, to know Him as friend and Lord is truly the only way that we can begin to scratch the surface of following Him. It is both the first step in being a disciple and all the steps combined. Jesus says it far better than anyone could.

> *"Love the Lord your God with all your heart and with all your soul and with all your mind." This is the first and greatest commandment. And the second is like it: "Love your neighbor as yourself." All the Law and the Prophets hang on these two commandments."* (Matthew 22:37–40)

We so often, just like the Pharisees, miss the forest for the trees.

The most important fact that we can take away from the early disciples is that they were *with* Jesus, every day, in everything. They were not just listening to Him, but they were practicing *(with varied effectiveness and results)* what He Himself was doing. They *knew* Him! They knew the Man in the flesh. They loved Him more than they even realized themselves. Day by day, their devotion grew. In over three years of life, not just what we would call ministry, but daily life, they became His disciples.

The point of discipleship to Jesus is often missed because the Man Himself is left out of the equation. Yes, His teachings are good. Yes, He did incredible things. Yes, He was the most enigmatic character in all of history. However, none of this matters, absolutely none of it, if we are not connected to the resurrection life of the Man Himself. If we do not love Him, we are not His disciples. If we do not love others because of His love for us, we have missed the design of Christ's approach to life entirely.

The point we are trying to make here, at length, is that Jesus is the end goal of discipleship. All else flows from this.

Let's take a look at the actual phrase, *"You miss the forest for the trees."* This essentially means that there is a larger problem at hand, the forest, and instead of seeing the entire picture, we choose a tree to stake our claim on and say that's what Jesus meant—whether it's a version of the Bible, how the poor are helped, in what way the church should flow in the gifts of the Spirit, or in what order the end of all things *(and its glorious beginning)* will take place or is taking place. These are trees. They are not the forest.

Our *"larger problem"* is how to live a life that is worth living—a life of value and purpose. If we stake our claim on some smaller part, we will miss out on all Jesus has to offer in following Him. We miss the forest, and oh what a wonderful, unending, beautiful, forest it is. We are offered an entire Kingdom, and we settle on arguing over the sticks and stones.

A Life of Discipleship

Discipleship is not a principle, or a set of studies, or a particular teaching to follow. Discipleship is a life. To be more precise, and also more expansive, it is a life in Christ. It is only in realizing this in our hearts that we can actually live alive for Him.

Jesus said, *"I am the way and the truth and the life. No one comes to the Father except through me"* (John 14:6). This passage gives us an insight into discipleship, into the *Way,* that needs to be brought to the forefront of the Christian life. I've always read this phrase, until recently, as a beautiful piece of poetry. On the contrary, it is not poetry; it is a phrase to actually live by. Not that poetry isn't something to pay close attention to, but when I say poetry, I mean just a nice thing to say that makes people feel a certain way but has no real concrete value in our daily lives, where real action is required.

"This is a nice phrase, Jesus, but what do I do now?"

This is where we can see how deeply religion has infected our belief in Jesus. We are looking for something to do when Jesus is clearly showing us a person. Even better, He is showing us a family.

What really is the essence of discipleship? What is the central substance of the Way?

Family—a family with a Father who loves them enough to send His treasure, His very essence, to die and live for you. All of this He gave to you so that you can inherit all of creation with Him and enjoy Him without shame. This was the original plan and purpose of God, and it still is. It is a way into what we have been looking for from the very beginning of our lives: The family that was shattered at the beginning with sin, then infected with shame, has been restored in Him and Him alone.

What kind of family is this?

A family that continues to multiply the goodness and glory of God on Earth through destroying the works of the devil—the work of the devil to divide by tyranny, religion, and materialism and to divide families and hearts—and setting captives free. *We* are called to follow Jesus, our older Brother, in eradicating the evil and malevolence Satan unleashed in the garden when Adam and Eve first sinned.

What then is our hope?

Our hope is in Christ and in Him alone to bring about the re-unification of His family under one Name. Why?

Because Jesus is the only one worthy to do so. The greatest sacrifice, the truly living one—Jesus removes all shame and doubt about who the Father is and what His desires are for us, opening the door to His Kingdom where we can live in true freedom, with a new name and a new identity.

This is why we must be reborn, to be renamed in this new family as one of His redeemed ones.

You see, discipleship is so far from a program that to call it this makes it a sick joke. We have enough programs, and services, and meetings, and talk. What stands before us is the very living Word that turns the chaos of our hearts into order so that we can find, not only the peace in our hearts that He gives, but peace with others. How?

We must keep the end goal of discipleship in mind. To follow Jesus is to have unbroken fellowship with Him and to obey Him. It's that simple. And *"being discipled"* means pointing your whole life toward doing what Jesus says and getting as near Him as possible, with every fiber of your being, because He is alive. A living Jesus tells us now, and forever, that following Him in the way brings us into this new family—a family worth fighting for and a family worth spending our lives for.

So, we violently pursue Jesus, the encapsulation of the Kingdom itself.

We now see why the Kingdom of heaven is so violently opposed and requires violent men and women to advance it. If indeed the family is restored through discipleship to Christ, doesn't everything else begin to fall in place?

Think of the most painful and the most joyful experiences of your life. Look back to what has really changed you, shaped you, molded you, and gave you your identity. They were all relational.

If indeed we are made new in order to follow the Great Commandment that is given to us, discipleship to Jesus is the way.

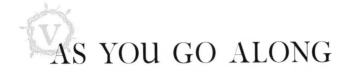# AS YOU GO ALONG

> "And behold, I am with you all the days,
> until the completion of the age."
> —*Matthew 28:20b Berean Literal Bible*

Human beings were designed to live in the present and also to make designs for the future. Although many of us can get stuck in the second part, trying to live in all the possibilities and unfortunate anxiety of tomorrow, the future, as tempting as it is to think so, is not a place where we can actually, practically live. We were made to live right now.

When someone asks how it is that they can become a disciple, the best answer is to be one right now in whatever they're doing, whatever their occupation. I mean this not in the sense it's normally used, like a job. I mean whatever occupies you at the current moment. Hopefully, it is reading this book, but when you put it down, what does being a disciple look like?

It looks a lot more like *"as you go along"* than *"What will I do tomorrow?"*

Every day is made up of innumerable moments, but how can we possibly know how to be like Christ in every single one of these? The first part of the answer is to be in the moment we are actually in, especially when it involves our relationships. How are you treating the person right in front of you? Whether it be your daily, set aside time with Jesus or your conversations with family, friends, and co-workers throughout the day, how is Jesus present with you in what or who is currently occupying you?

In a day when distraction reigns, when our brains are literally trained to find something new, to open an app or a webpage, to bounce from one thing to another, teaching ourselves to simply be in a moment and see the Kingdom in it can seem like an impossible mountain to climb. The good news is we don't have to do this alone, and we don't have to do it all at once. We can live in the Kingdom with Jesus on a moment-to-moment basis as we go along.

The one thing that we can begin to expect from life is the unexpected, so we must be ready for this inevitability. How do we go about our daily lives doing this? How do we keep ourselves from being completely overwhelmed by the task at hand of being like Jesus in a world that is going precisely the opposite direction in almost every way?

We must become people of the Presence. It seems like the early disciples had some unbelievable superpower available to do the things that Jesus had asked them to do. At times, I think it's a little unfair that they got to literally walk with Jesus and watch Jesus go about His life and ministry. Are we really expected to change the world like they did without the physical Presence of Jesus with us on a daily basis?

Yes, we are, but we also have exactly what they have: the Presence of the Spirit of Christ, the Holy Spirit, working in and through us. As Jesus said to His disciples, *"But very truly I tell you, it is for your good that I am going away. Unless I go away, the Advocate will not come to you; but if I go, I will send him to you"* (John 16:7).

We have the eternal Holy Spirit, yes, the one who hovered over the waters, brooding over the earth at the beginning of creation, living with us and through us on a daily basis. This is why Jesus is so confident that we can fulfill the Great Commission that He has given us. It's not by our own power or strength, but by the same Spirit that raised Jesus out of the grave. Through Him, is how we will do it. This is how we will remain, on a day-to-day basis, in the very moments we exist from minute to minute, completely aware of God's plans and purposes that He wishes to fulfill. This grand plan to restore humanity to God happens in our daily lives, and we get to be a part of it, if we can just learn to pay attention.

Pay attention to what? Here is a better question, pay attention to whom?

Living this life the way Jesus commands us is having a living, breathing, lively relationship with the Holy Spirit. There really is no other way. We cannot expect to attain to any level of real change in ourselves, or in the lives of those around us, by our own efforts. This is complete futility and has led many a good-hearted Christian down a road of frustration and eventually resentment.

"God said He would be with me, so what is going on? Why aren't we

having the impact that is so clearly revealed to us in Scripture that we are called to have?"

The answer has always been a person, *the* Person.

Any Christ follower worth his salt, the kinds that books are written about or the kinds that have books written about them in heaven, has always practiced the *Presence.*

Think of the unbelievable goodness of this. God, the God, the only God, the Lord of heaven and Earth, the consuming fire, Lord of Angel armies, with power and love beyond comprehension, dwells within you in every moment of every day. We just need to stop for a moment in our racing hearts and minds, and pay attention.

This does not come easy, it seems, at first; but in time, it can become better than second nature. In fact, it will become our nature itself. We can actually get to a place where Jesus is directing our every moment, even when we sleep. What a day to live in, what amazing opportunity lies before us to fundamentally change the way we live and the lives of those around us.

Now our Western minds immediately jump to, "How do we do it?" It's practical to think this way. If you're on one side of a river and living the way Jesus intended you to live, fully alive with resurrection power within you—literally oozing out of you in every moment and ready to catalyze and sustain transformation—you naturally want to build a bridge to the other side and know how to build it.

So, here is where things just get immensely backward to our normal way of thinking. We simply cannot build that bridge. It is not in our power to do so, although it is in our power to choose to know the Bridge Builder. The point is that the bridge has already been built. The Holy Spirit gives us the eyes to see it and to cross it. To live this new life will mean being a completely different person. All we have to do is walk across the bridge that has already been made for us. Paul said it this way, *"For we are God's handiwork, created in Christ Jesus to do good works, which God prepared in advance for us to do"* (Ephesians 2:10). Tozer said it like this:

> *The sovereign God wants to be loved for Himself and honored for Himself, but that is only part of what He wants. The other part is that He wants us to know that when we have Him we have everything—we have all the rest.*[1]

The whole idea is not to do something, but to know Someone. The doing will come most easily when we realize who Jesus really is. The apostles were with Jesus for His three years of ministry, they didn't really know Him, in a sense, until they say Him resurrected. It was then that the doing became clear. This Man whom they walked with daily for so many years was really who He said He was.

We waste our time pursuing knowledge without experience. Sure, we can have the whole Bible memorized front to back, but if we don't realize that the whole thing is revealing a person, we have missed the point entirely. We have literally read a book about someone who is in the room with us 24/7 yet fail to look up and see what He is doing now. As we mentioned before, it's a poor question to ask, *"What would Jesus do?"* A better question is, *"What is Jesus doing now?"* This is where knowing the Person of the Holy Spirit can transform our daily lives. The relationship is with the Person.

We can study, and fast, and pray, and listen to podcasts until we are blue in the face. We can practice spiritual disciplines, even do the right things, but miss the best thing.

You see, it is a walk-through life with Jesus, step by step, moment by moment, day by day. Tomorrow is far from guaranteed, but your connection to Jesus is sealed with blood. Choose the thing that cannot be taken away from you, and you'll find as you go along that opportunities to change the world will happen all the time. In fact, it will be overwhelming to you how much the Holy Spirit cares about the people you interact with on a daily basis. There is an inexhaustible supply of Jesus to give out to those who need Him and are desperate for the good news.

What should you do about your marriage?

Who should you pray for today?

Who should you share the gospel with?

What kind of miracle does God want to perform through you today?

What do you need to repent of, right now?

The answers?

Every single one is found in your relationship with Jesus.

The simplicity of this is somewhat frustrating to people, like me, who would just rather be given their orders and go and do them. Unfortunately for us, total dependence on Christ is the only way to live this life.

> *"As you go, proclaim this message: 'The kingdom of heaven has come near.' Heal the sick, raise the dead, cleanse those who have leprosy, drive out demons. Freely you have received; freely give."* (Matthew 10:7–8)

It's unfortunate how convicting this short phrase from Jesus is. How few of us answer the call to do what He asks us to do each and every day. This is what life is meant to look like. Jesus says the Kingdom of heaven has come near.

"Okay, prove it."

Great, I will, by healing the sick, raising the dead, cleansing the lepers, and driving out demons. Nothing so clearly proclaims the arrival of the Kingdom than the power of the Holy Spirit eradicating the works of the devil.

For a long time, this has been the life I desired, although for some reason I always placed in it a tomorrow that never came. If I could just be changed *"enough,"* holy *"enough,"* disciplined *"enough"*—if I could just cross that bridge to the other side where these men lived with Jesus, living in the midst of the way of the violent, proclaiming the Kingdom and attesting to it with signs and wonders. The day never came. Something was deeply wrong with the way I was approaching this life. The answer, I found, was not to look to tomorrow for Jesus to do some miraculous work and change me, but to completely rely on Him and His Word, today.

It seems simple, but many times the most profound things in this life are simple. It's when we complicate our walks with Jesus that things start to nosedive.

It was never about tomorrow, the Kingdom of heaven is here right now, and there is only one door. We choose each day to walk through it, to pursue the King of kings and get all the rest thrown in. He is the treasure hidden in a field, and all of heaven and Earth comes with Him. The inheritance that He promises to share with us, this new life, is all in Him—where our programs, plans, and scheming all fall short, Jesus meets us, flat on our face in the mud, and tells us to stand up, look around, and do what He's doing right now.

When all else fails, He makes this promise to us to never leave us, and it's at such a time that the promise takes on its unbelievable glory. Never leave us, never forsake us. Our imperfect, toddler-like stumbling through this life takes on a wonderful grace that our heavenly Father truly delights in, not because we are so good at what He asks us to do, but because He simply takes delight in us. It is in His delight in us that we realize, through our daily relationship with Him, how He allows us in his Word and character to do the good works He prepared in advance for us to do.

How good is our God?

Too good to even contain in a lifetime of pursuing Him. *Thank you, Jesus, that we have all of eternity to enjoy God.*

When our work is done. When this way of Jesus culminates in our physical death, our lives have just begun. But as we go along our way in this life on the earth, we've been given our ups and downs, the victories and defeats, and our joys and heartbreaks. Jesus, our friend and Lord, is right there, showing us the way.

So how do we get to know this Person?

Simple. Like a child, and on purpose.

THE WAY OF THE VIOLENT

"If you have not chosen the Kingdom of God first, it will in the end make no difference what you have chosen instead."

—*William Law*

All of our lives, daily pressures push against us like an invading army. Every day we wake up, we feel the constant strain of all the mental voices. What will you do about your relationships, your money, your position, your status? How will you respond to the day laid out before you?

The world around us seems to be tearing itself apart at the seams, while at the same time the human heart suffers the same fate. Billions of hearts split apart and shatter to pieces by tyranny, consumerism, and religion. Starving people looking for a scrap will sacrifice their own hearts just to get a taste of life.

This is why Jesus goes directly for the heart. The way of Jesus has always been a way of the heart. Where does real life happen anyway?

Right there, in what we call the heart, the center of real human decision making. Yes, logic has an important part to play. The things that truly matter in life tend not to make sense logically but are the only things that help us make sense of life at all in the end. The friendships we hold dear, the wife we love, the children we raise, the experiences that bring us sheer joy, the Savior who dies and lives again—these are the things that help make sense of life. What does this tell us about human beings?

That we are creatures of the heart.

Jesus so often teaches in parables because people understand stories, not in the way you'd understand a factual question with a factual answer like 2+2=4. We understand stories on a far deeper level. They reveal to us what life really means because stories speak to the heart.

I assure you, to live the life that Jesus promises will require far more than throwing up a prayer now and again and hoping for the best. Entering into the Kingdom of the heavens requires an all-out effort supported by all-sufficient grace. In one of the classic paradoxes of following Jesus, it requires complete surrender for complete victory. This may be the hardest thing we ever have to do, to simply say, *"You're right. I'm wrong. I can't do it my way anymore."*

Jesus offers us no other way.

Why?

Because He loves us.

As strange as that may sound, with all the intense language that

Jesus lays out before us and the expectation of extreme action to apprehend the Kingdom, He knows that nothing else will do. That gnawing sense inside all of us that says, *"There is more. What are you waiting for?"* Only a truly loving God would answer that oh-so permanent question plaguing the human heart: *"I do not feel like this is 'it,' so what is it that I am looking for?"*

The clearest and most wonderfully simple answer is Jesus, the Man Himself.

What every person longs for in their heart is someone who knows them completely, accepts them, and loves them enough to make the greatest sacrifice to ensure they know just how much He is willing to give for their freedom.

In the Kingdom, you are not just forgiven of sin, but set completely free to live life, and life to the full. Do possessions do that? Can religious adherence do that? Is what you're doing now, providing that?

Of course not, but that's why you picked up this book in the first place.

When it comes to entering the Kingdom, the only way in is through—through the Man Himself, Jesus of Nazareth.

Final Thoughts

There were a number of times where I thought maybe I should pull back on the title of this book. Perhaps the theme was too strong or the way that I approached the writing was overly aggressive. Now that I'm sitting here late at night (the only time two boys under two allow for writing), I don't think I was.

Entering the Kingdom of heaven is not a process of half measures and compromising choices. It truly is a life of sheer violence—of full-tilt rebellion against the ways of the world and all the cheap imitations of God that it throws at you.

We carry our cross and die with Christ.

We are baptized and resurrected in Him.

We live life by the awesome power of the Holy Spirit.

When we are hated, we love.

When we are spit upon, we delight in the privilege.

When our reputations suffer for His name, we rejoice that we are His.

All said and done, there is one goal and one aim of those who choose to walk this path and are called by His name: unbroken fellowship with Christ.

He is the aim, the goal, the point, the beginning, and the end. We cannot fail to see that Jesus didn't come to make nice; He came to make war on the devil, to set the captives free, to bind up the brokenhearted. For us to realize this life, before we can join Him in this great work, we are the first to be set free and healed.

It is with this constantly renewed idea in our hearts, that we cannot, and do not, save ourselves—that a loving God gave all that was precious to Him and rose from the dead so we could have new life in Him, and then we can transform the world.

The world may say there are many ways to God. Unfortunately, for these other religions—these ways that call Jesus a teacher, a prophet, or nothing at all—they never reach their desired end: the greatest sacrifice, for the greatest good, eternal life. This is not in the sense that we just live forever in some kind of heavenly haze, but that we have eternal life *now and forever*. The passage of time forever and ever would seem far more like torture than a gift from God. Life, real life, is not just time passing; it has a different substance altogether. Everyone knows this. This is not the eternal life Jesus speaks of. He teaches and shows us life, and life to the full.

It is the creeping thought that sneaks into our minds that death is unnatural, things in this world are not right, and they are certainly not as they seem. We know we have some part to play, we know that the world around us contains so much more than the physical reality that we experience with our senses, and we know Jesus is the only shining light that truly points the way, that shines so that we can see clearly what is really happening right before our eyes—that the Kingdom of Heaven suffers violence, and the violent take it by force.

ENDNOTES

Introduction

1. "People don't buy WHAT you do, they buy WHY you do it." Simon Sinek, *Start with Why: How Great Leaders Inspire Everyone to Take Action* (New York: Portfolio/Penguin, 2009), 41.

2. "From business to politics, manipulations run rampant in all forms of sales and marketing. Typical manipulations include: dropping the price and running a promotion; using fear, peer pressure or aspirational messages; and promising innovation to influence behavior—be it a purchase, a vote or support. When companies or organizations do not have a clear sense of why their customers are their customers, they tend to rely on a disproportionate number of manipulations to get what they need. And for a good reason. Manipulations work." Sinek, *Start with Why*, 17.

2 You Don't Get Crucified for Being "Nice"

1. David Murrow, *Why Men Hate Going to Church* (Nashville: Thomas Nelson, Inc., 2011).

2. Ravi Zacharias, Twitter post, November 20, 2013, https://twitter.com/ravizacharias/ status/403333034134364161?lang =en/.

3 The Trinity of Evil

1. S. C. Curtin, M. Warner, and H. Hedegaard. "Increase in Suicide in the United States, 1999–2014." NCHS data brief, no 241. Hyattsville, MD: National Center for Health Statistics. 2016. https://www.cdc.gov/nchs/products/databriefs/db241.htm/.

5 The Death of Tyranny

1. "Invictus" was written by William Ernest Henley in 1875.

2. United States Holocaust Memorial Museum. "Introduction to the Holocaust." Holocaust Encyclopedia. https://encyclopedia.ushmm.org/content/en/article/introduction-to-the-holocaust (accessed on October 30, 2020).

3. Wikipedia contributors, "Excess mortality in the Soviet Union under Joseph Stalin," Wikipedia, The Free Encyclopedia, https://en.wikipedia.org/w/ index.php?title=Excess_mortality_in_the_Soviet_Union_under_Joseph_Stalin&oldid=985721991 (accessed October 31, 2020).

4. "Abortion Statistics." Rtlofholland.Org. https://rtlofholland.org/abortion-statistics/ (accessed October 30, 2020).

6 The Tyranny of Religion

1. The temple model—holy men, holy Book, and holy place—are constructs borrowed from a message series by Andy Stanley called "Brand New." It was published by North Point Resources in 2015 and available at https://www.rightnowmedia.org/Content/Series/230978/.

8 A Violent Passion

1. From *Perelandra* (1943). Wikiquote contributors, "C. S. Lewis," *Wikiquote,* https://en.wikiquote.org/ w/index. php?title=C._S._Lewis&oldid=2845982 (accessed October 31, 2020).

9 How to Die So You Can Live

1. Principle 10 from Chapter 11 of *The Art of War* attributed to the ancient Chinese military strategist Sun Tzu.

10 Lions in the Church

1. "Occupational Injury Deaths By Gender U.S. 2003-2018 | Statista." 2020. Statista. https://www.statista.com/statistics/187127/number-of-occupational-injury-deaths-in-the-us-by-gender-since-2003/#:~:text=This%20statistic%20 shows%20the%20total, deaths%20in%20the%20United%20States (Accessed October 27, 2020).

12 As You Go Along

1. "71 A. W. Tozer Quotes | *Christianquotes.Info.*" 2020. Christianquotes.Info. https://www.christianquotes.info/ quotes-by-author/a-w-tozer-quotes/ (Accessed October 30, 2020).

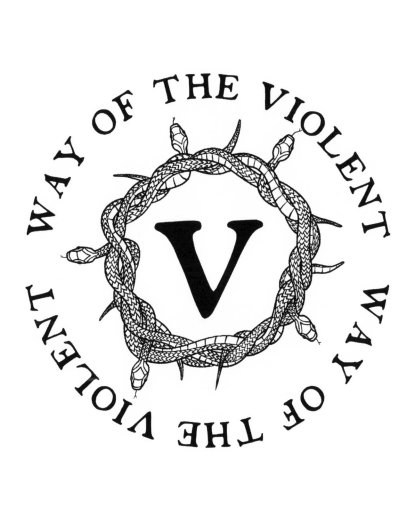

ABOUT THE AUTHOR

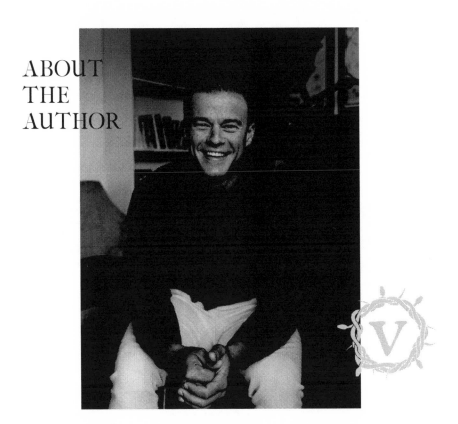

Parker Green is a father, disciple maker, church starter, preacher, author, and slightly above average crossfitter. In his eyes, belief in Christ has become softened to a degree as to almost completely lose its value to men. Only truly saved men will save societies.

Parker lives in southern California with his wife, two sons, and a daughter. For more information, resources, or to invite Parker to speak go to *thegreens.co*.